You're A Stepparent
...Now What?

You're a Stepparent

...Now What?

A Guide to Parenting in Families with Nonbiological Children

by JOSEPH CERQUONE

NEW HORIZON PRESS   Far Hills, New Jersey

Requests for permission should be addressed to:
New Horizon Press
P.O. Box 669
Far Hills, NJ 07931

Cerquone, Joseph.
        You're A Stepparent . . . Now What?:
        A Guide to Parenting in Families
        with Nonbiological Children

Library of Congress Catalog Card Number: 94-066761

ISBN: 0-8828-129-6
New Horizon Press

Manufactured in the U.S.A.

1998 1997   / 5 4 3

*With love and appreciation
to Henry and Palma Cerquone,
the world's best guides
to parenting.*

ACKNOWLEDGMENTS

The author offers deep and heartfelt thanks to several sources: Jeffrey Robbins and Dennis Hunt for their insight and support; the Stepfamily Association of America in Lincoln, Nebraska for being such a helpful cache of information; Paul C. Glick for his invaluable statistics; and stepparents across the country. Though approached "out of the blue," stepdads and stepmoms would always discuss their family lives with a ready spirit of cooperation, honesty, dignity and humor.

"You're writing a book about stepparenting?" many stepparents asked, amazed that a perfect stranger had called and expressed an interest in their lives. Then they would say: "Good. More information is needed out there," or a similar declaration.

Hopefully, this book fills the gap in guidance those good people detected.

CONTENTS

AUTHOR'S NOTE

This book is based on both my experience and extensive interviews with nonbiological parents. In order to protect the identity of others, I have changed some people's names and identifying characteristics.

FOREWORD
DENNIS J. HUNT, PH.D.

In new situations, the best way one can reduce stress and increase the chance for success is to know what to expect, and how to deal with it.

Learning by trial and error can cost heavily in emotion, energy and time, producing acute frustration. With non-biological parenting of children who have already had the experience of family life with other parents, poor advance knowledge and preparation can make their new parents feel caught in a "Rubic's Cube" living arrangement. They can puzzle over and manipulate the pieces for hours, weeks, months, maybe even years, yet never quite get them to align. Discouraged, these foster, adoptive and stepparents can erroneously conclude that they are in nothing less than an impossible predicament, when this is far from the truth; they have just not had the good fortune to know ahead of time how to succeed.

This danger makes it vitally important for new non-biological parents to understand the problems they are likely to encounter, identify their solutions and then pursue those answers with purpose and direction.

In a stepfamily context, especially going aimlessly about the business of trying to rear stepchildren is simply an invitation for trouble, as the emotional stakes in stepfamilies are quite high. Children may not have resolved their feelings of separation and loss with respect to the absent parent, and the couple heading the household may not have fully worked out their own relationship. Their attitudes and feeling about ex-spouses could be just one potential sorespot, for example.

Many stepparents have also never been around children. Consequently, they may not have realistic ideas about how to handle them. This may be complicated by spousal disputes over discipline. Haphazard tinkering with such deep and charged issues can trigger needless distress for all concerned—stepparents, stepchildren, parents and children alike.

Thus, I am pleased to say that in *You're A Stepparent... Now What?*, Joseph Cerquone has managed to provide new stepparents, and by extension, other parents of non-biological children with a well-lit path through the "terrain of the heart" looming before them with striking similarity.

The author's insights and his sensitive treatment of the subject derive, in part, from his years as a foster parent to foreign-born children. Foster parenting, as well as other forms of non-biological parenting, involves many of stepparenting's challenges, and all require special preparation and commitment.

As this book attests, Mr. Cerquone's first-hand experience of being a non-biological father has opened his eyes to the secrets of stepparenting success.

The three factors which are key to this kind of success are realistic expectations, a strong relationship between the couple and agreement on childrearing practices and roles.

Often, disappointment and frustration result from expecting too much too soon. Stepparents in particular, but also foster parents and parents by adoption of older and foreign-born children, are prone to tripping over this stumbling block.

When new families form, there are necessary losses and many varying pressures bearing down on them to make life right. Maintaining patience in this atmosphere, and letting relationships unfold naturally cannot be overemphasized. Quite rightly, Mr. Cerquone tells us that real success in stepparenting must be earned.

Also, the author brings attention to an often overlooked and misunderstood truism: it may be wiser for stepmothers and stepfathers to aim for respect instead of love from stepchildren, since the children often struggle with conflicted feelings about their new living situation.

How is a stepfamily going to make it if the adults are at odds or out-of-touch with each other? Furthermore, another fundamental but often overlooked point which this book makes very clear is that it will be quite difficult for a stepfamily to make it if the adults are always at odds with each other. The explanation of how and why actions by adults, as a couple, help determine the fate of stepfamilies is indeed worth noting.

New stepparents can feel overwhelmed when trying to figure out how to begin relating to family members. Children may be angry and confused and compete with the new spouse for attention from the biological parent. They may be testing out the new family situation to determine what the rules are, and how far they can push their new parent figures.

Such issues can undermine productive communication among family members and drain energy from the couple's nascent relationship.

In just one of his many timesaving tips, the author notes that the person they should worry about most is their mate. This excellent point is characteristic of the many gems of advice in *You're A Stepparent . . . Now What?* which can spare readers a great deal of emotional vacillation.

Mr. Cerquone has also provided an overview of legal and financial issues, including many important practical questions which all stepparents need to examine closely as they pursue the sensitives business of establishing their relationships with stepchildren.

In addition, there is valuable coverage of the somewhat awkward but critical matter of how to integrate ex-spouses; grandparents; and, in the case of other nonbiological parenting situations, other extended family members into the new stepfamily systems. The importance of these people in the psychological life of non-biological children, and the need for the non-biological parent to support such contact is stressed. After reading such advice, the anxious new step- or non-biological parent should emerge better oriented toward and more relaxed about their role.

For me, one of the most compelling aspects of *You're A Stepparent . . . Now What?* is its appreciation of the need for humor. To be sure, practicing humor in stepparenting is not to be confused with being silly or negligent. Rather, it is a useful way of retaining a healthy perspective and venting some of the frustration that can often develop.

As someone who has seen plenty of stepfamilies professionally—and who has been in a stepfamily himself for many years—I know of too many instances involving problems which were surmountable, but the people involved looked at them too rigidly, a mistake which ultimately undid them. With teeth clenched and jaws set, they tried grimly—and in vain—to come up with answers. Yet, had these stepdads and stepmoms just relaxed, they might have gained the comforting perspective that stepparenting is inherently difficult, and that it is perfectly natural and reasonable for them to feel challenged.

As author Cerquone points out, stepparents need to find ways to lighten up at times so that forging and managing their relations with stepkids is not such a dour—and self-defeating—business. *You're A Stepparent . . . Now What?* is one of the few stepparenting books I have read which has not overlooked this very basic piece of wisdom. In effect, the author suggests that humor will break the tension and renew one's courage to try again. And who can argue with his point?

Meanwhile, the format of the book complements its content. It is organized so that readers will more or less come upon issues in the general order in which they can expect to face them in real life.

In addition, there is no inflated or puzzling terminology which is meaningful only to clinicians. Mr. Cerquone writes in plain English, but in an interesting and entertaining style.

His anecdotes about Grace and Bobby—stepchild composites—are quite memorable teaching tools. Readers will recall them, and the valuable points their actions illustrate, for a long time to come.

Also, the use of quotes from stepparents about their personal experiences brings issues to life and makes the insights and suggestions in this book more credible. The device should give new stepparents courage, because they hear real people talking about matters that they will quickly recognize in their own situations. Indeed, it helps struggling stepparents to know that others have faced the same problems as they have, and have overcome them.

you're A Stepparent . . . Now What? has a remarkable life to it, for it is the type of book one can refer to time and again. Neither text nor fluff, it can be read by stepparents, and other non-biological parents, in the spirit of taking a personal refresher course.

The advice given is unique in many ways. It gets into the mind and hearts of stepchildren, unlike that in other books, explains their perspective in order to help new stepparents be as understanding and effective as possible.

Also, You're A Stepparent . . . Now What? has the capacity to be useful to a cross-section of readers: new stepparents, obviously, but also people like birth parents, grandparents, step-grandparents and other step-relatives, adult "outsiders" and others who may have to know what is happening with new stepparents and stepfamilies in order to act as an appropriate support network.

This guide is, in effect, a life preserver for the nervous new stepparent. Pack it like you would valued gear if you were heading into the great, but unknown, outdoors, for indeed that is the journey that new parents of non-biological children take. Bear in mind, however, that it is not a panacea (nor does it claim to be).

Certainly, if stepparents feel they cannot continue handling seemingly endless and complex problems, they should not delay seeking outside support and counseling.

Two excellent sources are stepparents who have "been there"—for example, people active in stepparenting associations and groups. Typically, they are dedicated to listening to others and offering them helpful interaction, moral support and helpful resources.

Another good source is local mental health associations. Through them, one can find professionals who are experienced, trained counselors in stepparenting issues. Periodically, too, these associations offer excellent classes, seminars, presentations or discussion groups—many times free—for interested parties. Usually, the dates and times for such events are in newspaper community calendar listings.

After reading You're A Stepparent . . . Now What?, the stepparents' new world should seem less mysterious and more negotiable. In fact, the importance of disseminating the truth about stepparenting cannot be underestimated.

Men and women need partners, and there are too many kids around the world who badly need effective parenting. Violence, the pitfalls of making it in a complex and uneven economy, the threat of AIDS, and similar factors can make the world a very scary place for young people, especially those who must adjust to new family situations and sometimes even new countries and cultures.

It would be comforting to think that millions of stepkids are not simply being "written off," but are coming home to happy, confident stepparents. Yet, the people I see professionally and in my personal experience tell me that, while stepparents are a very large segment of our parenting population, few of us want to acknowledge they even exist.

The roles of stepfathers and stepmothers have been de-emphasized and misunderstood for far too long, Mr. Cerquone indicates quite correctly. You're A Stepparent . . . Now What? brings the challenges, rewards and importance of stepparenting into a new light. With this book in hand, competent, committed stepparents will have a greater opportunity to build strong, healthy families in which children will find the emotional support they need to grow into well-adjusted adults.

I hope readers enjoy it as much as I did, and that, above all, they glean as much from it, too.

—Dennis J. Hunt, Ph.D.

INTRODUCTION:
A LOOK AT STEPPARENTING

Over twenty million men and women are parenting children who are not biologically related. As well as divorced parents—who are only the beginning of the story—this includes foster children whose birth parents are alive, older children adoptions, children of foreign birth, surrogate parenting and open adoption, in which lines of communication with the birth mother are kept open. One-third of the population belongs to a "step situation" and there is reason to think more than half of the men and women across the world today have been, are now or will be in one or more step situations at some point in their lives.

In the case of divorce, startlingly high statistics are virtually certain to keep turning up, too. Divorce rates are high and lasting marriages are uncommon. Stepfamilies, a term which will be used in this book to designate the many increasing forms of nonbiological parenting, will be one of the leading family forms by the year 2020.

Indeed, stepparenting is an important job. More and more, it is the children of stepparents—not those from the vanishing "nuclear" families of old—who will dash across our playgrounds, occupy our classrooms, assume posts, positions, and offices. For many stepkids, their views, values and attitudes—their very ideas of family—are going to be shaped by their new, blended families.

Divorce statistics are but the oldest chapter of the stepparent story, however; diversity marks the rest. There are stepparents who have taken foster children into their home, married women or men with children, adopted children from foreign cultures who still maintain some contact with their biological parents, women who parent the children of their husbands and a surrogate mother and those who choose open adoption. Some are stepfathers who parent kids at home, others are stepmothers who have not been married before and those who parent visiting stepchildren. Within those divisions are stepfamilies with only one set of children, others with two. Many new families form after divorce or death. Other combinations of parents, children and circumstances abound.

Nonetheless, commonality is mixed in with the diversity. Therapists, counselors and others who see the different faces of stepparents, and listen to their stories, say many of the problems are the same.

One way or another, virtually every stepparent deals with many of the same basic set of issues. Among them are adopting proper expectations, including preparedness for something other than a traditional family; establishing relationships with stepchildren; dealing with a partner's ex-spouse or birth family; disciplining stepkids; parenting stepsiblings; and coping with other parents, grandparents, holidays, and special occasions. These are the issues this book will address.

One universal truth about stepparenting is that while it can succeed impressively; it can also be complicated and difficult. Patience, perseverance and time are paramount.

Stepfamilies must adjust quickly to survive. Unlike childless first marriages, when a young couple is just getting started and has time before taking on parenting responsibilities, you must hit the ground running. From day one, your stepchildren are going to be challenging you at the same time you are working out your relationship with your new partner.

In an article titled "Children's Development During Early Remarriage," author James Bray notes that adults in stepfamilies have almost twice as many stressors than those in other families. It is no wonder. Beyond your direct relations with your stepchildren, there can be numerous potential pitfalls—dealing with ex-spouses, changes in income and job status, moving, decreased family cohesion and less effective communication and discipline practices. Thus, a loud chorus urges stepparents to be prepared.

You're A Stepparent ... Now What? is based on extensive research with many varieties of families. This book will do its job if it prompts the stepparent to check his or her expectations in the clear light of reality. Stepparents and stepchildren who can understand and accept that they are not going to match idealized images of family life stand a better chance of succeeding.

If you are a stepparent, it may help you to know now that perfection is usually not in the cards that you hold. The task you have taken on is much too complicated for that. Even on the road to success, you are bound to hit more than a few bumps—hurt feelings, jealousies, whatever. One long, smooth, ideal ride will not be your fate. For some stepparents, the journey may prove tolerable at best

And, it may comfort you to know that stepfamilies represent a continuation of family life throughout the world, irrespective of contrary public perceptions. Society is doing everything it can to make you feel abnormal, unacceptable and isolated. It is trying to deny the significant changes which are literally overhauling family life stem to stern.

Politicians campaign on so-called "traditional" family values, school practices fail to include stepparents, talk shows hype and broadcast unseemly and unhelpful stepfamily shouting matches and our legal system gives stepparents no rights.

"In their eyes, stepfamilies are against family values," laments Richard Victor, a Michigan lawyer who has actively tried to remove the jackhammer-resistant blinders covering officialdom. No wonder Norma, a stepmom who also counsels stepfamilies, says that "among stepparents, a common problem is that they always talk about the bad—they never discuss the good.

"But stepfamilies are not the oddballs some would have you think, not by a longshot. Stepfamilies have been around for a very long time—much longer that society will admit—and in fact, may be the 'norm' if you take a sweeping, realistic look at the history of family life throughout the world. Leading sociologists say high death rates desertion and separation caused by economic necessity often meant that, until the recent past, children were unlikely to spend all of their early years with both natural parents. In other words, if you are a stepparent, you have long, long line of kin. There is nothing wrong with *you.*

"People come in frantic," reports Maryland therapist Mala Burt. "They feel like failures because they don't understand that stepfamilies are different. They mistakenly take their stepkids' behavior personally."

But according to Burt, "Their anxieties usually ease when I indicate the normality of their discomfort."

Also, don't think your status as a stepparent automatically dooms you to failure. Family structure is closely associated with childrens' behavior, but it alone does not determine outcomes. More and more, researchers say success at parenting largely depends on several factors—not just the way a family is made up. Many stepparents and stepchildren are happy—even very happy. You and yours can be happy, too.

With the right approaches, stepfamilies offer heightened awareness and sensitivity to others, exposure to and appreciation of diversity and acquisition of an extended family network—a luxury in this era of shrinking families.

"We aren't the Brady Bunch," Angela, a stepmom says, referring to the idealized television stepfamily of some years ago. "But we don't have the problems everyone thinks we do, either." Her honest, balanced and reasonable view may be something to keep in mind as you turn these pages.

PART ONE...
GETTING READY FOR THE ROLE

"I'll never forget my wedding day," said Louise, reminiscing about her start as a stepmom. *"When I glanced at my fourteen-year-old stepdaughter, I immediately became put off by the way she was looking at me—her face had an expression of absolute rage. It shocked me. We had always gotten along; up to that point, I was sure my stepdaughter liked me.*

"Later, when I asked her what had been the matter, she explained that she and I had always gotten along because 'Dad was on his best behavior' while I was dating him. It hit her during the wedding that a big change was actually coming; she feared losing the good times for a regular household where good times were not going to necessarily be the norm.

"The fear that my stepdaughter didn't express— but what was also the case for her— was, 'I realized I was losing my position as Dad's best girl.'

"The last thing she wanted was another parent."

Stepparents know something about themselves other people don't: unlike the uncaring characters often drawn by literature and media, stepparents have blood running through their veins, not ice, and their hearts burst with good intentions, not schemes.

However, stepparents can be *too* well-intended. In plenty of real-life stories, people crash on stepparenthood's curved road because they hang blinding stars in their eyes.

"Unrealistic expectations are the biggest risk," warns Emily Visher, stepmother, psychologist and founder of the Stepfamily Association of America. She states, "Stepparents want to believe everything is going to settle down quickly, everyone is going to love each other right away. They try to force things into a first family form."

Chances are pretty good you will run the risk Visher talks about unless you check yourself first.

Impossible expectations are generally a continuing source of family tension. In some stepfamilies, the problem is between the husband and wife and is intensified and includes the children. Adults who are burned by divorce and death, often crave a shared happiness that has proven elusive. Pressure builds for stepfamilies to be perfect as couples kiss their pasts good-bye and new partners hello at lightning speeds. Lost in the process are opportunities to address and settle important issues pertaining to separation and loss.

"The time between divorce and remarriage averages less than three years, and 15 percent of children of divorced parents acquire a stepparent within a year," notes therapist Carole Webb.

Reality can barge through the door in several ways. Stresses and strains can start to surface from arguments with disruptive ex-spouses, financial pressures, and upsetting custody fights, to name just a few possibilities.

Meanwhile, after the newness of the family setting wears off (which can happen quite fast), people can start to feel confused by the ambiguous nature of stepfamily relationships.

Early on, stepparents often feel "out"—excluded by virtue of the natural bonds between parent and child. Many grow lonely and resentful of the deep, easy relationships of blood relatives. Stepmothers, in particular, often suffer in silence.

"My fantasies were pretty wild," recalls Linda, a stepmom, about the bliss she anticipated following her marriage to a man with a nine-year-old son, Jason. "Automatically, I thought we would be a unit. I expected everything to just fall out and clarify on its own."

But guess what? The common ups and downs of stepfamily life began to take hold. Everyone had to experience a normal, unavoidable period in which they worked out their relationships.

"It probably took a year before I recognized that I was not happy," Linda says. "I was feeling separate from the rest of the family. My husband had this relationship with his son, and I had one with my husband.

"But my stepson and I were strangers living in the same house. We didn't talk; instead, we communicated through Dad. If I was cooking and my husband and stepson arrived home, my stepson would ask my husband what was for dinner. There were plenty of instances like that. It was as if a rope was attached to my husband, and my stepson was pulling one end of it, and I was pulling the other."

Hurt and frustrated, Linda gave up on herself and became resigned to failing.

"I would shut myself into our bedroom and read," she says of evening after evening spent in self-imposed isolation. "I thought I was the problem, because I hadn't had children before. I worried that I wasn't being accepting enough towards my stepson."

Linda says matters began to resolve after she attended a stepfamily conference and realized she was normal since "other people were feeling like me." She says it helped, too, for her son and her to admit their true feelings about each other, then accept that "neither of us was going to go away."

On the other hand, stepchildren can feel threatened by the formation of a new stepfamily. It can destroy some big fantasies. By coming on the scene, a stepparent can very well upset the dreams that stepkids have of their parents getting back together, or it may loosen the exclusive hold the stepparent had on his or her new partner.

In the stepchild's eyes, such "accomplishments" may not recommend the stepparent to live with them under the same roof. Stepparents had better be perfect, stepkids might grumble: loving, supportive, kind, smart *and* good-looking, among other traits. Even if the stepparent fulfills all of those requirements, it may not be enough to reassure and pacify their stepchildren, at least right away.

◆　　　◆　　　◆

It is easy to moralize and say that stepparents should chuck any dreams they harbor of a perfect stepfamily. Exactly *how* are they supposed to adjust their outlook?

A good starting point is adopting a patient parenting style. In effect, stepparents should keep their dreams in check but allow themselves and other family members to break with the past, figure out where they stand with each other, form new relationships, and decide where to go as a stepfamily. All of that takes time.

Stepparents can do their part by encouraging members of their stepfamily to acknowledge and express their fears and insecurities, and to openly confront, discuss, and work at venting whatever guilt, anger, and other strong feelings they have. Being patient and tolerant as a stepparent will help enormously in this area. One shouldn't be offended, though, if stepchildren are comfortable confiding in their parent only at first—that would be normal. However, as stepkids detect their stepparent's good intentions and the two begin to bond, the stepparent may be able to take a more active role. Should you partake in any family discussions, encourage people: not to be ashamed of how they feel—feelings don't have to be right or wrong—just true; to let go of guilt or blame—neither produces solutions and both can be harmful if they are blown out of proportion; to hold on to the good in their past—no one is saying that the past was a total loss—there were good things that should be recognized and appreciated; and to have a positive, forgiving attitude towards themselves and others. By being open and honest, your stepfamily will have an advantage in resolving losses and accepting its inherent ambiguity and complexity.

None of this is easy. Stepparenthood is "almost like the pain of birth . . . You are creating a new life together," wrote Katherine Barrett and Richard Greene in a *Ladies' Home Journal* article titled, "A Stepfamily Christmas."

The value of perseverance cannot be underestimated. Stepfamilies can take as long as seven years to feel adjusted or "family like," according to Patricia Papernow, a therapist who has identified distinct stages in their development.

In fact, Papernow so respects the period that is needed to recognize needs and close emotional distances between and among family members that she warns stepparents against using the term "blended family." In her view, the term implies a hasty whitewash. "'Blended family' is a cruel phrase," Papernow asserts. "If a new family has blended, someone probably got creamed."

Benefits Do Await

Most likely, many new stepparents will have hope for the following as they try to adjust to their new lifestyle:

- They will have a dream house with the picket fence, only a few years later than they thought.
- Their stepchildren *will* hug them, grateful at last for the many times they gave the children spending money, or rearranged their schedule to drive them to one of their many extracurricular activities.
- The day *will* come when they can march out their front door with the distinct feeling that they aren't weird, that what goes on in their house approximates what goes on behind every other home on their street.

Even with a more realistic outlook, such things cannot be expected. Little is automatic. A lot depends on timing.

"Stepparenting largely depends on how and when you come into the life of your stepchildren," therapist Rene Norton of Cincinnati notes, referring to a point she says frequently gets overlooked, "If they are under age six, you can expect to be a parent to them, but if your stepkids are older, you are looking at having another kind of relationship."

Norton continues: "In effect, biological mothers' and fathers' nurturing of their children allows them to parent. If you haven't been the nurturer, the child won't feel you deserve the same entitlement."

According to Norton, a stepparent can expect the length of the bonding process to be equal in years to the age of the child at the time of their first encounter.

In stepparenting, gratification is redefined as well as delayed. Stepfathers and stepmothers tell few stories about getting tangible, immediate payback. Instead, their experiences are aptly characterized by the maxim "virtue is its own reward."

A growing sense of closeness from travelling a hard road with your family; the pride of overcoming odds; a sense of accomplishment from reaching an inter-personal high-ground where you and family members co-exist reasonably well: such are the payoffs when a stepparent sets better goals.

If that isn't all you hoped, think again. Through effort and determination, stepparents can play a key role in *creating* a very special parent-child bond. Many who take on that task discover a unique sense of satisfaction that is never experienced by the natural parents.

In addition, it can make a big difference in the course of the stepchildren's lives. The successful stepparent and happy stepfamily can be important sources of stability. They can ease the pain and confusion children feel when their parents part ways.

Beyond that, by good example, a stepparent can subtly open his or her stepchildren to broader, more diverse ideas about people and human relationships, teaching them to be more accepting and understanding.

They can show them that it *is* possible for individuals with divergent backgrounds, without obvious reasons to get along, to get live together on reasonably good terms.

The stepparent can be a model of the importance of effort and the wisdom of taking nothing for granted. During a temporarily muddled and disappointing time, they can serve as a beacon of understanding, respect, generosity, forgiveness and maturity.

These are not small lessons or gifts for stepchildren—or any kids—to learn and appreciate.

The Couple Is Your Guide

The confusion new stepparents feel is often attributed to a lack of "blueprints." Unrelated by blood, family members come together with different pasts and customs. People can have widely divergent feelings or expectations, and very different states of mind. One cannot expect family members to adjust at the same rate, however. Moreover, the usual indicators which tell other kinds of families how to function together are missing in these new situations.

Who has authority? Who is disciplinarian? Who is *entitled* to determine the kids' bedtimes and weekly allowances and the drivers of the family car? Answers are automatic in traditional families, courtesy of blood ties. Children accept parents as enforcers without question.But what if someone does not have a ready-made bond with the kids? Why *should* a stepchild listen to a stepparent? How are roles and responsibilities going to be sorted out among family members?

Mistakenly, some stepparents try tending to the kids along traditional lines. However, they usually discover those methods are not applicable to their situation, and are therefore ineffective.

The good news is that complete "blueprints" aren't necessary to be good at stepparenting. For openers, all a stepparent has to worry about is teaming up effectively with his or her new partner. A couple's commitment to each other and to their relationship is very significant—much more critical than issues like discipline and finances.

"The conjugal unit is most important in the stepfamily," says Deborah Witt, a stepmom and researcher. Witt spent part of the early 1990s asking contented stepparents to reveal the secrets of their success. What did she find? There's one secret: a strong couple.

"They told me they needed to be united, committed to their relationship," Witt explains. "They agreed to disagree, and to talk about ideas before they presented them to their kids. Communication was very important."

Witt's research mirrors what she has discovered personally. According to her, the fact that she and her husband Ron have never "allowed the children to divide us" is a major reason why they have remained married for years, regardless of having to care for six stepchildren of widely varying ages. "The kids have a tendency to pull at you, but we just stick together," she offers.

What kills unity? Any number of factors. A partner may hold back, feeling guilty about putting the children "second." Or there can be other forms of distraction and divisiveness: rivalries between stepchildren and stepparents for a parent's attention; stepsibling competitions; emotional, financial and custodial pressures dating from previous relationships; difficulties adjusting to the newness lining everything, from a residence to a partner's parenting style to money arrangements to extended family members.

"It can be very chaotic at the beginning," according to therapist Mala Burt. "Crisis inundates the new marriage and the couple is constantly in the position of being distracted with fighting brushfires. Typically, they can't find time to nourish their relationship."

But find time they must. Stepparents and their spouses must make sure to break from the grind regularly, together and alone. This is a simple remedy, but one that will require active planning and commitment during the hectic early days of stepparenting.

Taking a trip to Paris is not required. However, for many harried stepparents, even a few minutes away from the daily grind can seem as tough to manage as an exotic vacation.

Stepparents and their spouses should try getting to-gather after the kids are in bed, or simply taking a walk. It is important to designate space and time at home for these respites—the bedroom or the family den, for instance—and to let everyone else in the family know that this private time is sacred. Parents and stepparents can also try to merge portions of their daily schedules to see if they can combine business and pleasure. For example, if they are sitting in the bleachers watching a child's ball games during the coming weeks, perhaps they could schedule their talks for then.

If a couple really feels ambitious and wants to change its routine a bit, meeting in town for coffee might be a good idea. If money is no object, a weekend getaway here and there would be a perfect way to spend time together. Another idea would be scheduling a vacation while the kids are away at camp or visiting the outside parent.

Whatever and however they are managed, the breaks will be invaluable to a stepparent's sanity. Often, step-parents fear failure. They tend to worry ceaselessly and, many times, needlessly. By checking in with their partner continually—by each asking about the other and getting the other's perspective—stepparents can put such fears to rest, take some pressure and guilt off themselves and improve their outlook. In general, checking for false expec-tations will revive the "truth" about the identity and purpose of the stepfamily, and will help stepparents and partners reach and maintain an understanding about goals.

Also, couples can use such interludes to conduct calm, honest discussions of such other important issue as how to resolve the past, relations with ex-spouses, house rules, disciplinary techniques, new traditions, conflict resolution and financial concerns. The parent would then have time to listen sympathetically to the stepparent and plan ways to keep him or her from being the target of stepchildren acting out negatively.

Conversely, spending time together can also prevent the adults from resorting to scapegoating. When stepparents fail to discuss their problems and insecurities honestly, sometimes they can pick on stepchildren instead of confronting fears, pinpointing real sore spots and looking inward for answers.

Finally, at an even simpler but nonetheless important level, the time-outs can be a chance to relax and forget life's stresses while nourishing a new relationship—no small achievement, given the many distractions which can arise in the course of daily life.

Will private time stall or prevent cohesion in a stepfamily? Actually, the opposite should happen. The breaks will foster and rejuvenate couple unity, a vital ingredient of any stepfamily. In that sense, these respites will foster family togetherness, prudent and necessary, rather than selfish and divisive. Without a well-functioning couple, any stepfamily's chance to last is sharply compromised.

FAIRNESS, NOT LOVE

Catherine, a stepmother, tells a story about her "saddest day":

"At the time, my stepdaughter was still living with us," she recalls, "but she had started to rebel. Her mother couldn't care for her, since she was travelling a lot. Well, when I confronted my daughter one day on her behavior, she completely blew up at me.

'I hate you, your kids, and this house!' she yelled. 'I never want to come back!'

"I felt angry and hurt. But there was something else, too. At that moment, it hit me that we were never going to be *this big happy family. I had gone into things thinking every-thing would be great.*

"When that turned out not to be the case, it was dev-astating. I couldn't believe that my stepdaughter was so unhappy. I was in my thirties, I had been through a divorce and I still had blinders."

Driven by fear of failure or the high standards of part-ners trying to make up for the past, many new stepparents set out to be "Supermom" or "Superdad." However, this troublesome approach can blind stepparents to what rela-tions with their stepkids are really going to be like. And when truth hits them, as it did in poor Catherine's case, step-parents can be in for a distressful letdown.

Some people naively assume that their stepchildren will love them. Others expect to be at least liked and appre-ciated. Often, though, neither happens. As a result, step-parents fall into bitter funks, thinking of the times they "do for those ungrateful children," in big ways and small: weed-ing dirty clothes from obstructive heaps and washing them; helping with their homework late on weekday nights: hold-ing off and ordering what the kids want for takeout, just to keep an uneasy peace.

Soon, such thoughts can shift in content and focus. Upset, some stepparents may have self-recriminating feel-ings with an inner chorus shouting, "You aren't fit to par-ent! Wouldn't these kids, who have known pain and loss, head straight for your arms if you were?"

Such a victimizing attitude is the product of one of the biggest myths around: namely, that stepparents and stepchildren should feel the same about each other as par-ents and their kids do. Commonly, stepparents and step-children don't love one other at first. And even over time, love often fails to bloom. For most, it is a fairly remote possibility.

In other words, you have taken on the wrong role if you are looking for love at first sight from stepchildren. Fairness and respect, not love, are the standard for all parties in early stepparent-stepchild relations.

"A stepparent must walk gingerly," cautions Dianne, one stepmom who says it took nine years for her to develop a closeness with her stepson. "The best you can hope for is mutual respect or friendship. Unfortunately, too many stepparents expect instant love and set themselves up for failure."

"The media asks the wrong questions," laments Emily Visher, co-founder of the Stepfamily Association of America. "They want to know whether stepkids love their stepparents. It is not realistic to expect that."

Why is this so? One simple answer is that kids never forget their fathers and mothers. They keep their love for them and them alone. When the stepparent arrives on the scene, stepchildren can experience severe loyalty conflicts, especially if their absent parent is deceased. They can shut off the stepparent, thinking that to enter any kind of a relationship would betray their absent parent.

These feelings can be strong if the stepchildren are from a marriage which ended in death. Stepkids may idealize their deceased mother or father and reject a new union as a disrespectful blow to that person's memory. Results of the Harvard Child Bereavement Study, recently reported in the Washington Post, stated that "children need to maintain a sense of connection with the [deceased parent] for their own developmental purposes . . ." But none of this may occur to the rejected stepparent. "I expected them to appreciate me, since they know what it is like to lose a parent," the disappointed stepfather or stepmother may think. "But they don't. What ingrates!"

Meanwhile, as stepparent and stepchild size each other up, it may turn out that love or even goodwill does not come from your half of the relationship, either. To adults, stepkids can represent a lot of unpleasantness. They may remind the stepparent or their partner of a past of divorce or death that they both would just like to forget. Often, the kids come enmeshed in custody arrangements that drag a hostile ex into a fresh new life, and they can easily become targets of resentment.

Fortunately, relationships with stepchildren are hardly hopeless. There are several things a stepparent can do to avoid crushing a disappointment and to make these ties reasonably rewarding.

First, as a stepparent, be supportive of your stepchild's relationship with the "other" parent. Accept the fact that you cannot become an "insider" right away by replacing that person. If you understand that feeling like an outsider purely reflects the nature of early stepfamily life, you will gain valuable and useful insight. You can achieve the ability to have a relationship with your stepchildren that is unique and stands on its own. You will not feel the need to be in a draining and debilitating competition with anyone else.

Secondly, create a new role for yourself. You don't have to be a "parent," per se. Numerous other possibilities exist. They include acting as an uncle, aunt, godparent, babysitter or simply an adult friend. (If your stepkids are very young, however, you may find success as an active *additional* parent in their lives.)

Practice what Marion, the mother of two older stepchildren calls "detached warmth." You should be always interested, open and aware of what is going on with your stepchildren; you should be empathetic, non-defensive and non-judgmental; you believe in them. But you should also adopt a less active parenting style than your partner.

You should not come on so strong that you appear to be forcing yourself down your stepkids' throats, or acting like a phony. This type of behavior should be far less intimidating and confusing for your stepchildren and you will stand a better chance of winning their trust and goodwill. Stepparents who focused on being just friends with their stepchildren speak of the kids coming to them with problems they otherwise might have hidden. With an objective, uninvested, non-threatening stepmom or stepdad, the children were more open to adult perspective and advice.

In conjunction with these steps, lead your own life. It will help prevent you from becoming anxious about winning approval from your stepchildren or getting too sensitive about developments in your stepfamily.

"Things would have been better if I had interests of my own," asserts a Judy, a stepmother of two stepchildren, thinking about the sense of isolation she battled. "It is important for new stepparents to have hobbies and interests apart from their family life." Stepparents should not court burnout by focusing entirely on their stepparenting role. The marriage relationship should come first, and keeping up with other friendships and career is important, too.

As the adult in most cases, though, the onus for setting the tone and direction of a relationship with stepchildren is going to rest with the stepparent. To get things off on the right foot, it is necessary to find the proper moment to talk with a stepchild and to offer words like: "I realize you have a father (or mother) whom you love. I respect your feelings toward that person and I'm not interested in replacing the relationship you already have with them. However, I want you to know that I care about you, too. It is important to me that we get to know each other, become friends, get along with and respect one another. I will be here for you, so don't hesitate or be afraid to come to me.

My door is always open. I'm a good listener." As a non-threatening stepparent, you could then suggest that the child is really *gaining* something—a new adult friend in their lives—on top of the valued relationships they already have with their parents

Because some stepchildren are defensive, especially when a stepparent is new, several approaches may have to be made before receiving a positive response. But stepparents are urged to keep trying—to keep planting seeds, says therapist Mala Burt.

"Some come up and show through, others don't," Burt says. "However, the more seeds you plant, the greater are the chances some will grow." She attaches a key condition, however. "The behavior of stepparents must back up what it is they are trying to impart," she notes. "Many people fail to understand that."

Also, stepchilden may try to use stepparents' good efforts to "extort" things from them. Kids can sense a good thing and may try to milk friendly overtures for extra treats and privileges—especially if they are coming off of period of feeling deprived or disappointed.

Thus, stepparents could hear exaggerated reports of how well the kids live with the outside parent—accounts about how that person buys this or lets them do that. As an adult, you must keep your cool while not giving in to this particular power game that children can play. It is up to adults to determine standards of behavior—their parenting methods should not be driven by the pressures children apply. Bear in mind, too, that support from the original parent is essential in developing the stepparent-stepchild bond. He or she should not wield a "love me, love my kids" sword.

Rather, a parent should not pressure anyone—stepparent or stepchildren—to love anyone else. As a stepparent, you cannot be expected to feel the same as a natural parent about your stepkids. Furthermore, your partner should give the kids credit for sensing the different circumstances and emotions that distinguish stepparenting from parenting, reassuring them that the formation of your new stepfamily will not affect the love they have known.

Some factors are going to be out of a stepparent's control entirely. For instance, it helps to possess the good fortune of having well-adjusted stepchildren who have good relations with their parents. Many therapists believe children with a positive relationship with their parents have a better chance of getting along with their stepparents. Stepchildren with good attitudes and healthy personalities adjust more easily. Some children (and adults) have problems with new situations and people, including new stepparents. In a *Ladies' Home Journal* article titled, "Why Kids Act the Way They Do," writer Olie Westheimer revealed the findings of a study conducted by Dr. Stella Chase and Dr. Alexander Thomas. The study showed that sixty percent of all kids were either "slow-to-warm-up," "difficult," or some combination of those traits and the characteristics of an "easy child"—one who is friendly, happy and moderate in temperament.

If stepparents are aware of such findings, they will be less apt to automatically blame themselves when something goes wrong. The outcome of interactions with their stepchildren will rest on many factors—little will be cut and dried.

How to Deal with That Certain Ex

There are many sad stories of custodial and non-custodial homes at odds when it comes to rearing children. Caught in the crossfire of warring households, they have confrontations with ex's, or feel victimized and miffed by financial demands or childcare. As the adults battle, the children pay. In some cases, children are used inappropriately as hapless messengers between homes where people are not on direct speaking terms.

You can prevent some of this ugliness, as a stepparent, by maintaining a positive attitude and staying open to the chance of reasonable relations between families. If, however, this is not possible, try to focus instead on what is in your control, namely your own stepparenting techniques. As long as you do the best you can, you will have met your stepparenting responsibilities. Whereas, if you are predisposed to being hostile to your spouse's ex, chances are you will just intensify any existing ill will. Also, you will probably engage in an unproductive waste of time and energy. Fighting usually solves nothing, yet it takes much out of the combatants, and it could diminish them in the eyes of their stepchildren. Indeed, you risk setting a poor example for your stepkids—children who may have been already exposed to much incivility among adults.

A stepparent can implement a good outlook in several ways. Though primary responsibility in custody matters rests with the original parent, they could be encouraged to conduct good-faith childcare negotiations with the other household to preclude or ease conflict. Compromise is always best. No one can be bent on winning everything if everyone is going to get along reasonably well.

Because custodial and non-custodial households often have difficulty in communicating, stepparents may not know what rules to enforce when their stepkids see the "other" parent. Sometimes, children use this ambiguity to test a stepparent with rebuttals about what they are allowed to do when they are at their absent mother or father's. To counter, the stepparent must say something like, "That's fine when you're *there*—but our rules *here* are these."

It is crucial to stay flexible enough to adopt the rules the other household has, however, if they seem reasonable. In general, one should respect the other parent's rules and disciplinary responsibilities, too. Some kids talk negatively about what happens in one house to elicit sympathy or attention in the other. The wise and impartial stepparent should not overreact to or encourage this. Ideally, parents in both households should confer to minimize ploys by stepchildren and to erase disciplinary inconsistencies that might confuse them.

As a stepparent, it is up to you to show some understanding by not getting jealous over your partner's dealings with the ex. You will have to be trusting, accepting and secure in yourself. Your mate is going to have a lot to contend with if you live in a custodial household. In an article titled, "Child Care After Divorce and Remarriage," Frank F. Furatenberg, Jr. states that non-custodial parents assume very little responsibility for children, while, typically, custodial parents make the important decisions. You must realize that your partner has two co-parenting relationships, in effect: "one with the new spouse and one with the ex-spouse," according to therapist Carole Webb.

However, perhaps the most important message of all to stepparents is this: do not badmouth the ex in front of your stepchildren or try to "replace" a former spouse in other ways. Constant, sarcastic references to "your father" or "your mother"; using stepchildren to convey or obtain information about the other household; or acting upset, unhappy or jealous over reminders of the ex (such as gifts to the kids, pictures, etc.) are taboo. This behavior can erode your stepchildren's respect for and trust in you and also damage their self-image. After all, they are a combination of their parents, and hearing you be so critical about one may make them wonder if something is wrong with them.

You may actually have reason to complain. Some ex-spouses are difficult to deal with or show up unannounced and hang around the homes of their former partners when the children are there. Some stepparents have had to deal with sudden changes in custody arrangements and become almost overnight custodial parents through need or even selfish motives on the part of their former spouses.

Former spouses must respect the current home and marriage, and the stepparents should make this clear. In general, however, the stepparents would be wise to vent any negative feelings in private. (Time alone together for the sake of couple unity would be a good setting for this exchange.) If you must discuss the ex with your stepkids, be reasonable, balanced and objective. Harsh criticism or constant petty complaining will not serve them or your stepfamily's welfare over the long-term.

YOUR DREAM HOUSE

In the role of stepparent and new spouse, a good indicator of your expectations will be where you decide to live. Perhaps you or your partner already have a house which seems perfect. It has enough room and is in good condition. In light of the lingering upset of divorce, coming to terms with new children and seeing to the many other details that go with forming a stepfamily, sticking with the house you know seems a good, expedient choice.

But what appears to be a blessing could become a curse. Often, stepfamilies go wrong when they move into a place which was home to a previous union. The adult new to the scene never gets comfortable because, floor to ceiling, in decor or design—in "feel"—the home has the absent parent's imprint.

Meanwhile, the arriving children may resent not having a room as large or as nice as their resident stepsiblings, or it may bother them that they had to relocate from their neighborhood and school. Not only is "some other family" in their home, but they had to say painful goodbyes to friends besides!

The kids now in the house can turn hostile, too. Seeing newcomers in their home, the present residents may resort to guarding their "turf" jealously or ordering the new residents around.

Some stepparents, to minimize unease and squabbling, choose to begin their union in a new setting. If you can and do, everyone will stand a better chance of feeling like they are starting out as equals. Your dream home is the one which is brand new to all, free of reminders which can spark division and discord.

Occasionally, stepparents learn lessons the hard way. Planning a relatively simple move can often turn into a nightmare. Typically, many emotional struggles will occur. However, selling a home may take months or be virtually impossible. You may simply not want to let a place go at a lower price because you have other, burdensome financial obligations. What, then, is a good compromise?

Answers could lie in fresh paint or wallpaper, rearranged or reconfigured rooms or new furniture and carpeting. In short, some redecorating or remodelling can chase unwanted ghosts from a home that once housed a former marriage or relationship.

If you choose to do this, proceed carefully and collectively, though, especially if your stepchildren are grown and spent years in your home.

To be sure, you have a right to have your new residence look as you wish; it is yours. But in the interest of familial harmony, you will probably want to seek your stepkids' opinions first, or break news of impending changes to them gently and in timely fashion in order to reduce hurt feelings.

They may not have lived at home recently, but they may still regard your place as *theirs*. Sudden remodelling on your part could upset them. Robin, a woman who is a stepmother to a twenty-year-old stepson and two teenage stepdaughters, tells the story of a stepson coming home from college and carrying on for an entire weekend about changes she had made in his absence.

"The kitchen *wallpaper*?" she exclaims, incredulous that he picked a repapering job to be angry about.

You, the stepparent, may sense already that, no matter where you live, it will be important for people to have a niche which serves as a refuge for kids and adults in the unsettled first stages of your family. No matter where you reside, have at least some place where people can retreat to sort out feelings and insecurities or take a breather; a spare bedroom, a study or a basement recreation room might serve the purpose. Giving everyone an area as "their space" may be difficult, since stepfamilies are often big. You do not have to limit yourself to rooms only, however, any place appealing and functional may work just as well

In any event, discuss the choices with your family. After selections are made, clarify that they are strictly for the use of the persons concerned. Do the same for visiting stepchildren; it is a good way to make them feel and be a part of things. It only stands to reason that your family will have a better chance of adjusting if people are not made to feel like outsiders, trapped, on display or pressured to socialize and accept their new life before they are ready.

Privacy will be key in other respects, too. Your home may not be laid out so that it suits all the ages and genders of the children in your new stepfamily, but perhaps you can better plan the allocation of space so that teenage girls and boys are not in a removed part of the same floor, or next to one another. If two sets of kids of different genders are going to be under one roof, you should plan carefully where to put them.

Luck will be on your side if you move someplace where all the children have the same sort of room. But they may not, and there could be feuding. Kids who think they are being relegated to smaller, less appealing bedrooms may feel slighted and resentful. A solution may lie in setting up a schedule of rotating occupancy so that everyone eventually has a shot at the "good life" in the better rooms. And what about bathrooms? Will there be enough for the sake of convenience—and peace?

NAME, PLEASE?

Here is yet another typical scenario for stepparents to consider:

The day of the big move unfolds. Things are going smoothly. In a burst of enlightenment, you and your partner think through room assignments, but also give your children a say about them. Everyone seems satisfied.

Soon, however, there is an unsettling development. The last belongings are being brought in when a neighbor wanders over, having noticed your moving van. He extends his hand.

"Hello. My name's Bob Jones," he says. "Are these your stepchildren?"

Your well-intended neighbor is ignorant of this, but this ordinary greeting unnerves you. What are you to answer? As Jones stands there waiting for a reply, the larger repercussions of the question strike you, your family has not yet had a discussion about names. Are you a "stepfamily?" Are some of the children "stepkids?"

You hesitate to use the prefix "step." You don't like it. Years of unfair, negative connotations and stereotyping have exacted a toll on the term "stepparent." Somewhere in the back of your mind, it registers that *Webster's Dictionary* once defined a stepchild as "one that fails to receive proper care or attention."

Do family members want to conform and use one name? Or would they prefer to go with a hyphenated surname, or their own last names? Will your stepkids want call you "Mom" or "Dad," and be known as your "son" or "daughter?" And what about stepsiblings? To each other, should they be sisters and brothers?

It will be unfortunate if the answer you give to your neighbor upsets members of your family. But whatever you say to "Mr. Jones" will not be your first mistake. For many stepfamilies, never tackling such questions in the first place is the real problem.

Indeed, for the sake of clarity, there should be honest discussion about names even before a couple marries. Sometimes, despite even obvious differences in the appearances of family members, adults in stepfamilies slip into the practice of giving everyone the same surname, hoping to create an image of togetherness. The approach can be woefully simplistic—and potentially damaging. It can create resentment in your stepchildren and make your relationship with them worse than it would be otherwise.

The issue of names bears mentioning for other reasons, too. Young children with last names different from everyone else in the family can end up confused and feeling like outsiders, especially if their mother takes their stepfather's surname. On the other hand, some kids may resent a stepmother for taking their last name; this could be seen as a disrespectful attempt to replace their mother.

At the other end of the pole, you should think about some concerns of your own. Unaccepting stepchildren may avoid addressing a stepparent by name. This behavior can prove hurtful, erode self-esteem and become an obvious communication barrier which could have been precluded by having a direct talk in advance.

A guiding principle would be neither to assume nor to demand—and clear the air as much possible. Adopt usages which, within reason, respect everyone's wishes, personalities, emotional needs and ability to understand. Ask your stepkids point blank, with *their* feelings in mind, what they want, rather than expecting or imposing ways for them to address you or you them. (Encourage them to do the same with their new siblings, too.)

If you prefer being called Mom or Dad, but fear supplanting a parent, you may want to suggest a combination of "Mom" or "Dad" and your first name. It works in a lot of families.

As an aside, there is an answer for those heated times when you hear, "You're not my father (or mother)!" from your stepchildren. Reply that they are quite correct —you are not, that will always be the case and you aren't looking to change any relationships. But also add that when they are with you in your home, you and your mate are in charge.

Perhaps there will be no need to say that, though. If you settle the name question head on, with awareness and sensitivity, you may earn a place of respect inside your stepchild's heart. Still, remember that your relationship with your stepchildren will be the key thing to worry about. Dealing with names is important, but only to a point. In the big picture, addressing the question may help a little, but learning and understanding your stepfamily at a basic level will much increase your chances of success.

"They call me 'Dad' when they bring new friends over, 'John' when they bring old ones," a stepfather says of his stepkids' behavior. Gail, a stepmother from another family notes: "At school, my kids have three different names." The arrangement doesn't seem to bother her, though. "We are a family because we care for each other," she explains.

Although their lives sound confusing, these two people speak with amusement, even assuredness. To their credit—and their families' benefit—they appreciate the value of flexibility and humor. They realize that stepparenting is untidy in many respects, including names. "But so what?" these stepparents seem to say. They appear to have discovered the deeper lesson: it is not so important that the children use or have different names. In the homes of these stepparents, people find a way to get along, anyway. They have learned not what it takes to be perceived as a family, but what it takes to *be* one.

SPARING THE ROD

Discipline in stepfamilies requires the coolness of diplomacy as much as, if not more than, the heat of force. Many stepfathers, in particular, adopt "get-tough" policies. They think iron rule is the secret to handling stepchildren; in fact, some stepparents see their new partners as saviors and encourage their spouses to be strict. Frustrated and tired of the responsibility of disciplining, they look to men to produce obedient children by cracking the whip.

It is self-deluding, however, to think that handling the children is going to simply involve laying down one set of rules, administering swift and harsh punishment to anybody who doesn't obey, and then standing back and watching as your stepchildren come to attention in a neat, respectful row. Actually, calm, consistency and consequences—not agitation, shouting, threats or strictness—have been cited as the key ingredients of effective discipline. It is also simply erroneous to believe that a stepparent can be an active disciplinarian early in the relationship. By doing so, the stepparent could derail the family's development as a potentially cohesive unit.

Stepparents and stepkids share neither blood nor history. This disqualifies the sensitive stepparent from wearing a sheriff's badge around the house during the early days in his or her new role. (A deputy sheriff's badge would be more appropriate.) You will be much better off if you first develop friendship and then mutual respect with your stepkids— they will be much more inclined to accept discipline from you if they like you. However, until you break the ice with them and establish a bond, they will regard their parents alone as entitled to tell them what to do.

Thus, forget any ideas about laying down the law or leading on the disciplinary front. If your new family is the result of divorce or death, that job belongs to your partner. Some estimates say it takes two years or longer—approximately the time needed for a solid, friendly stepparent-stepchild relationship to develop—for stepchildren to accept discipline from a stepfather or stepmother

In successful stepfamilies, discipline and couple unity are closely linked. While stepparents should not focus on being prime enforcers, they should have an equal say in what goes on in their homes. In other words, you and your partner should be the ones authorized to establish rules, but you have to be ready to compromise. It may be quite possible that you and your spouse differ on ideas about responsibility, privileges, punishment and reward. If so, you have to figure out how to meld your different ideas together. Research indicates that agreement by adults on child-rearing principles is more conducive to effective discipline than the methods chosen to apply them.

So you and your partner should sit down and identify those areas where you want to see discipline applied. You may feel in the dark or overwhelmed, however, especially if you have never parented before. "Where does one begin?" you may wonder. Here are some suggestions for bewildered stepparents:

Overall, your new home should be a place where there is respect for everyone. Family members must be considerate of each other—they must respect each other's views, ways, beliefs, backgrounds, rights, belongings and "space." Their disagreements should be settled reasonably and peacefully. Politeness—saying "please" and "thank you"— must be encouraged, while back talk, sarcasm and profanity need to be discouraged. And, of course, people must learn to share

Because you are a stepfamily, it is very possible that your furnishings will be a mix of goods from the adults' respective households. One side of the stepfamily must respect the other's things. You may want to announce, gently but clearly, what the procedure will be if an item is broken, damaged or lost. That may sound stern, but your stepfamily may welcome such a rule; it could be seen as a form of insurance that will also prevent hard feelings between owners and careless users. In addition, the living space in your household must be respected. Everyone should pick up after him or herself, lend a hand in keeping your new home clean and know enough not to roughhouse indoors.

Work out the freedoms and the restrictions your mate and you want to impose. Will you have curfews? What limits are there going to be on use of the car, the TV and other electronics? What are your feelings about such varied topics as dating, sex, homework, religious practices, movies, eating, money, allowances and use of substances?

Will you expect all members of the family to attend special family functions such as holiday dinners? Will you require them to be present at gatherings given by your relatives?

Can visiting stepchildren feel free to drop by or stay with you anytime? What limits are there going to be on your stepchildrens' contact parents living elsewhere?

Sometimes, relations between stepsiblings can become sexually charged. Consequently, give thought to restricting their sleeping arrangements, access to each other's rooms, dress at home and times alone. As a general rule, all members of your stepfamily should practice modesty.

Think through the chores you expect your stepchildren to do. It will be much easier to assign them at the beginning, when everything is fresh, then to try to add them on later, when your stepkids may object that they are an unexpected addition to their responsibilities and thus, unfair.

Your stepkids' chores can include keeping their rooms clean and tidy and putting away their belongings, doing their own wash, keeping the car clean and the gas tank full if they use it, tending to pets, taking the garbage out, doing yardwork, babysitting, helping with general housework, grocery shopping and meal preparation and cleanup.

That is quite a list, and you certainly do not want to enslave your stepkids. However, assigning them some chores can teach them responsibility, make them feel like they have a stake in your new stepfamily and keep you and your spouse from feeling overburdened by your many new responsibilities.

If your stepkids are not used to doing chores, the prospect of daily tasks as part of their new life could seem pretty unappealing. Your partner and you may have success in gaining their cooperation if you present some choices and ask your stepkids what they prefer to do—for example, some children like pets and enjoy taking care of them. Or, you may choose to rotate the responsibilities to keep any one child from feeling stuck with a certain job and treated unfairly

Finally, put a premium on communication—this is always a good idea in any type of family. Have your stepchildren inform your partner (and you, if they can accept you) ahead of time of their plans, with whom they are going to be, where they are going and when they are returning. Going out without keeping an adult informed of their whereabouts, or straying from the watchful eye of a parent if the children are very young, should be prohibited.

✦　✦　✦

Whatever you do, remember that "perfect" kids are not a realistic goal. This does not mean to expect little of your stepkids or pity them because they are "stepchildren." (That would be condescending to unfair stereotypes which portray stepkids as inherently defective. This does mean, however, that you understand and accept the fact that you had no role in their formation until now, so you will accept their present behavior as not reflecting on you. Thus, you neither set yourself up to feel guilty or embarrassed by their wrongdoing, nor make the mistake of taking it personally. In other words, you have a clear sense of your real place in their lives, and theirs in yours.

Instead, at the beginning, you may want to focus on just a couple of areas for having things done your way or seeing evidence of obedience. Rather than trying to change your new world immediately, keep your personal goals or wishes modest—aim for or be on the lookout for such small bits of order as making sure all the videos are picked up around the VCR or keeping the bathroom clean and free of clutter. That way, you will feel like you have some power and influence, yet your expectations will be realistic and stand a fair chance of being realized. Furthermore, your self-respect is not endangered should your stepchildren fail to obey.

Once you and your partner agree on rules and how you want the children to behave, set goals for each child. Come to an understanding about which actions you will praise, punish or ignore. Track what the kids do to make sure everyone does their job and no one feels burdened.

Overall, your mate should express support when you discipline so that you avoid looking like a "mean ol' stepparent" in the eyes of your stepkids. You both should meet *as a couple* with your stepkids and discuss impending changes in rules. Your legitimacy will be enhanced if your mate prefaces matters by saying something like, "We have decided that we would like to have to the following rules . . ." Indeed, when it comes to discipline, the importance of couple unity can not be underestimated. It makes a dramatic impact.

Conversely, let's say a parent gives in and allows a young child to stay up later than usual. The decision is not conveyed to the stepparent who discovers the kid stretched across the den floor at 10:30 on a school night. The tube is turned on to some made-for-TV cop movie. However, in real life, "Stepparent: DOA" is about to begin with a bang.

"You should be in bed by now," or some such mild remark is barely out of your mouth before you are blindsided with, "*Mom* said I could stay up." Suddenly, you appear like an overzealous cop to a child whose sense of victimization may already be high. Moreover, you seem unaware of decisions being made in your own home; you look "out of it"—barren, in effect, of any real authority. This sort of breakdown in couple communication may not appear like much of a problem, but it is one of those minor snafus that can balloon into "major deals" in the fragile atmosphere of a new stepfamily.

In a recent *Ladies' Home Journal* article by Margery D. Rosen titled, "My Stepchildren are Running My Marriage," a stepmom grumped, "We talk about what the rules should be concerning homework or having boys over and agree on something, and then Pat [her husband] just doesn't follow through. He tells me yes, but he really means no." This woman was so upset and frustrated, she feared for her marriage. Too many little things had been allowed to build up; for too long, her stepfamily had been operating without the benefit of good couple communication and commitment to a unified front. Unfortunately, her sort of predicament is not unknown to other stepparents as well.

A mother or father may fail to discipline because they are wracked by distorted feelings of wanting to "make things up" to the kids. Consequently, they either exempt their children from rules or let them get away with misbehaving. Gradually, tensions build until finally there is a major argument. Or, by default, stepparents are thrust into the awkward position of disciplinarian. Even worse, they may discover that they have all the responsibility, but no authority. Their partners may take to correcting them or being unsupportive. A parent may even side against the stepparent in front of the kids. If that happens to you, you could come off looking rather unimportant in the eyes of your stepchildren, and feeble as a disciplinarian.

That the parent is supposed to take the lead in applying the rules should not leave the stepparent so vulnerable however. You remain entitled to respect and support from your spouse when the rules aren't followed—and at all other times, for that matter

"Wimpiness" isn't respected by many people, including stepchildren. While you should hold off as a disciplinarian at first, there are going to be instances when you need to lay down the law. Do not shy away from this task. Some stepparents are uneasy about being firm with their stepkids because they want to avoid alienating their new partner or being accused of favoritism if their own kids are living with them. They fear failing, a big mistake in all aspects of parenting. Stepparents think if they punish their spouse's kids, they will be disliked, though they usually are not.

One tip—when those moments do come when *you* have to be the adult who reminds your stepchildren of the rules, express your actions as being representative of you *and* your partner's wishes, rather than just your own. That way, avoiding appearing to "butt in where you don't belong," or making yourself an easy target for back talk or defiance. Constantly communicate with your mate on disciplinary matters. Use your private time together to confer about handling the kids and to review, modify or change disciplinary approaches and techniques altogether. By communicating in a constant, coordinated fashion—use the phone, answering machines and handwritten notes, if you must—you can guard against confusion and power plays and your stepkids will be less able to "divide and conquer." Broadly speaking, the degree of couple unity will signal your dedication to and seriousness about your stepfamily. That not-so-subtle message may contribute mightily to helping your stepchildren behave.

To be sure, sometimes a "bad fit" fuels problems—there is trouble because of a clash in temperaments between stepparents and stepchildren. Your stepchild could also have a behavioral disorder, complicating matters further If this situation becomes your predicament, evaluate it realistically and with detachment. You may have little choice but to accept the fact that you are going to be in for tough times. Among the worse things you can do are blame yourself or fall into despair. Both behaviors will solve nothing, and either one could erode your self-confidence as a stepparent, hampering your new family's development.

Over the long run, your stepchildren may grow out of their problems and be just fine. But if a negative situation persists, you and your partner should consult a professional counselor, have the child evaluated and then, based upon that testing, pursue treatment accordingly. However, it is also true that if you discipline at the beginning of your relationship with a defensive, prejudiced view of your stepchildren as burdens or enemies— as a blight on an otherwise perfect new union— they will sense your negative attitude and probably behave accordingly. In significant measure, people act as they are treated, and stepchildren are no exception.

Take some risks and some time to see, know, treat and believe in your stepkids as good people. Credit them in the beginning of your relationship, with being interested in behaving, as long as you and your partner hold up your end by applying discipline uniformly, consistently, clearly, honestly, imaginatively and—above all—fairly.

If you haven't parented at all before this marriage you may want to get some outside advice about discipline. With your partner, take a course on parenting with local stepfamily association chapters, civic groups, churches or social service agencies. More than the more experienced stepparent, you are going to have to check that all-important meter: reality. An ocean of change awaits people who enter stepparenthood straight from the adult single world where things are scheduled, organized, remembered, neat, budgeted, and serious.

Children are truly wonderful, but—like adults—they can also act silly, take the easy way out, waste time and play. They can be myopic, selfish and manipulative. A lot of people forget that when they discipline, they are laying adult expectations across young shoulders; or they are being completely naive about behavior of the children. On the other hand, don't fall too quickly for the stepchildren who cry "I wan to live with mom (dad)!" when discipline is applied. Indeed, your partner and you must be flexible and discriminating enough to consider revising custodial arrangements under certain circumstances. For instance, many stepkids want to live with the same-sex parent—and in one home only—when they reach their teenage years. But it is also true that stepkids can resort to experimenting with emotional blackmail with no real intention of going anywhere else. However, you should be aware of basic behavior patterns for children of the same age as your stepchildren.

These days, the opening and final shots of high-tech warfare are fired in less time than it takes some teenagers to get out of bed. If you are to have perspective and humor as a disciplinarian, you are going to have to understand such factors. You can not enter stepchildren's lives expecting them to behave with a mature adult's levels of efficiency, seriousness and care. If you do, you could very well end up deflated down to your shoes.

There persists an erroneous, almost subliminal assumption that getting children to mind only involves punishment, chastisement, criticism and denial. Fortunately, though, there is another side to this coin. Discipline also means encouraging, praising and building esteem, which many adults do not realize. Statements by you to your stepchildren such as, "I'm happy that we are a family," or "You are important to me," or "I believe in you," also will help them to know you respect and care for and about them. In the minds of many experts, praise is one of the best disciplinary tactics. Giving your stepchildren attention and extra privileges as rewards for behaving can be very effective.

Remember, too, that no matter what you do or say, part of a child's behavior is out of your hands. In one sense, parents have to discipline because their job requires it. Kids really do learn a lot from experience.

Money Matters/Finances

You are settling into an easy chair after a hard day when it happens. One of your stepkids—let's call him Bobby—is searching for you.

"Mo-o-o-o-om! (or Da-a-a-a-ad!)" Bobby yells.

Hearing him call you mom or dad makes you feel great. After all the organizing and reorganizing, ups and downs and uncertainties of your first weeks as a stepparent, your stepchild now sounds friendly, even anxious to see you. The real interesting part is that Bobby is actually using a term of endearment. Hey—the kid must *like* me after all, you think.

The sight of the boy awakens you from your reverie, though. He wears an unmistakable look; it says he wants something. He shifts his weight impatiently from one leg to the other, and he is silent in a strange, expectant way. His jaws work, but nothing comes out.

Finally, Bobby manages to speak. *"Do you have twenty dollars?"* Your face reddens as you take in your stepson's question. Do you have twenty dollars? Is that really what he said? This question is coming from a boy who up to now has largely treated you like a terminal disease.

Struggling mightily to be adult, however, you steady yourself and begin to ask some questions. It seems Bobby needs the money for a school excursion the next day that

he had forgotten about until now. As the only parent home—
your partner is away on business—you end up giving Bobby
the money he needs. He runs off with a curt, unfeeling word
of thanks, clutching a fistful of bills.

However, you are another story. Miffed, offended and
resentful of Bobby's lightning-quick cash draw, you fall back
in your chair and remind yourself that you have your own
kids to worry about. Just yesterday, *they* made similar
requests. In your pre-stepparenting days, you never expected your wallet would get such a comprehensive workout in
twenty-four hours.

Worse, there have been other times just like this when
money was needed and you were left in the position of
being the bank of first and last resort. Before long, it seems
to you that the whole manner of dealing with finances in
your new home is a screaming troublespot that can't be
left unattended another moment. Money and emotion are
tightly, even explosively, linked.

In truth, most stepchildren, like birth children, ask for
money at times. There is no cure for this parental role. But
there is something you can do from the onset as you build
the foundation for your new life, to preclude or mitigate
problems with monetary affairs. You must consult with your
partner right away and set up financial housekeeping.
Ideally, you should design a comprehensive plan to put
each partner on equal footing.

Adopting realistic expectations about personal relations, your choice and style of residence and other basic
issues such as names and discipline are effective steps in
making your new family work, but you must complete the
job, however, by figuring out how to address a range of
financial questions—from small ones like Bobby's, to big
ones—like estate planning and taxes. These matters are

bound to bear significantly on your new life. Money matters can be a major sorespot

Perhaps you will become well off by virtue of entering stepparenthood. However, if you do, you will be the unmistakable exception, for money is in short supply for most stepfathers and stepmothers. Many can't afford to be fiscally unprepared or foolish—for them, two dollars, let alone twenty, is meaningful.

In stepfamilies formed after divorce, new debts that come with having more kids to care for mesh with old financial obligations trailing back to previous lives. The resulting financial squeeze is one reason why most stepfamilies are at an economic disadvantage relative to other family types.

But that is not the full story. *How* money is used—as much as *how much* of it is around—is often the key issue. Stepfamilies that are otherwise happy can get stressed making tough, highly emotional decisions such as how to divide bequests between stepchildren and children.

One clear emotional time bomb are those stepfamilies formed after divorce where two sets of children are involved, the adults don't merge resources, their income levels differ and they have conflicting spending and investment habits.

The side of the family with money buys freely; the side without, scrimps and saves. Obviously, the former is "better off" than the latter. Perhaps worse, the disparity is evident. Soon, hard feelings well up and the stepfamily is split down the middle between haves and have nots. "Why should *my* kids be deprived, while *his* have everything?" or vice versa, becomes a common complaint.

But even when a couple is willing to share their resources, trouble may develop if their communication about money is poor. A mother may wonder: "Would it be better for my children if I continue to seek support for them from my former husband, or should I rely on financial help from my spouse? Wouldn't that strengthen the bond between my kids and their new stepfather?"

A parent may become guilt-wracked knowing the step-parent contributes to the children's welfare, while the absent parent never forks over a cent. Bobby's mother (or father) may be the last person to ever give him what he needs; financial problems, spite, disputes over divorce settlements, or simple neglect could be among the reasons why.

Then there is this scenario: let's say Bobby doesn't live with you. As the non-custodial parent, your partner worries about not being more involved in the boy's life, and is always giving in to his or her ex's demands for support which are over and above the terms of the divorce decree. You resent this because it is emotional blackmail and diminishes your stepfamily's resources for other things.

Bobby is indulged by the other parent, and the ceaseless flow of gifts and spending on him undermines you. Because all the attention distracts Bobby, you wonder how he is ever going to be interested in getting to know you.

Because many stepparents find themselves in these sorts of binds, you and your partner should discuss finances right away.

OPENING NEGOTIATIONS, FAMILY SPREADSHEETS

New stepdads, or in some cases, stepmoms, should not naively assume that their partner's children will be supported by the other birth parent under the terms of the divorce settlement. Failure to pay child support is a national scandal, and despite some attempts to round up "deadbeat dads," the fact remains that most people who owe aren't always made to pay. It costs money to find them, and officials are unsure whether jail time and fines turn the wayward into reliable providers. Moreover, for an ex-spouse, prosecution costs are often prohibitive.

If you are a stepmother, or in some cases a stepdad, you may have to live with another set of fiscal frustrations. For example, your husband or wife may have alimony payments to make. (They would terminate only if his ex remarries.)

Whether you are a stepfather or stepmother, make sure you figure on the potential for change in financial obligations (or at least pressure for change) if alimony and child support are in your stepfamily's picture. Rarely are parties satisfied over time with divorce terms. Lives change and people's needs, especially children's, change with them. In addition, some divorced couples may engage in running disputes over money to vent ill-will.

If you find yourself living with such turbulence, encourage your mate and his or her ex to consult a mediator and resolve things. That would free you and your spouse to plan your finances more accurately, get on with your lives, and be a model of reconciliation for your stepkids. For your own calculations, start with each adult's monetary obligations and income. Be sure you cover alimony, child support, prior mortgages, present and future educational costs, and any special forms of health care. Updating your insurance policies across-the-board should also be part of your financial housekeeping. And, if your expense sheet is going to be realistic, you need accurate information about your stepchildren, too.

What are they like? What are their attitudes toward money? What are they used to? Do they have costly medical conditions? Do they have interests or seek careers that involve intensive training? Do they want to be musicians? Athletes? Something less usual, but expensive to pursue nevertheless? Ask your partner for a full and honest run down.

Keep in mind the ages of your stepchildren and try to project ahead. If they are very young, child care expenses may be involved, or one parent may be needed at home, something which could take a chunk out of your income.

If you are the stepparent of teenagers, you may soon be facing bursting food budgets, buying cars and paying for auto insurance, college tuition and text books. If you have stepsons especially, your grocery bills could skyrocket. Some of these expenses can be handled with novel solutions. For instance, you may want to investigate belonging to a discount store where you can save by buying groceries in bulk.

Unfortunately, automobiles are more necessary than ever these days. You may dread the thought of your stepchild having his or her own car, but you may be pressured to acquire one more automobile to meet everyone's need for "wheels" after your stepchildren start driving. At the least, you will probably have to increase your auto insurance to cover the additional drivers in your household.

But would another car be affordable? Who would pay for it? Would you want your stepkids to contribute? When? And how? In one lump sum, or spread out like typical car payments? When you discuss expenses, be sure to look beyond the purchase price—figure in maintenance and insurance costs and any other taxes which apply in your area.

With respect to education, find out what will be your responsibilty. If you are expected to pay for a stepchild's college attendance, this could present an economic burden. If you are a new stepparent in a non-custodial household, you need to be updated on what plans, if any, your spouse has for sharing higher education expenses—which can become a pretty big issue between former spouses.

In fact, for adults in stepfamilies, a looming choice may boil down to this: either having money to send the kids to college, or having adequate retirement funds. Some experts recommend choosing retirement, while others just as adamently recommend choosing the children's education. In the end, the choice is yours.

Discussions about education often raise the same questions as those about cars. Will you contribute? How much? How? And when? Even if your stepkids live with your partner's ex-spouse, and your partner and his or her children have been incommunicado, you should have a backup plan for such costs in mind. After extended separation and silence, custodial parents have been known to suddenly "send the kids along to dad or mom" or do similar outrageous things once college bills begin to arrive.

Another set of "expenses" could come with adult stepchildren. Because of the tight job market, many kids are leaving the nest much later. They live at home and save until they feel more financially secure. If you support that kind of choice, do you expect your stepchildren to pay room and board or help cover household expenses? Does your partner?

Both of you should agree on the arrangement and present it as a joint proposal open to discussion and some modification. Figure in some lead time so your stepkids can budget—or decide to live somewhere else. To prevent resentment and awkwardness between step parents and stepchildren, if there is a birth parent in the home, he or she should be the one to make sure his or her children honor the payment schedule.

If you have adult stepchildren, be mindful that they may think they are entitled to property that was acquired during their parents' marriage such as heirlooms, furniture, equipment, cars, artwork, even a house. In addition, certain items may hold great sentimental value for them. For instance, if a former wife was a seamstress, her children may object to the idea of their stepmom using their mother's old sewing machine, especially if it is the same one she used to make many of their clothes when they were growing up. If Dad was a collector of some sort, your stepchildren may want a certain item he treasured as a reminder of 'Pop'".

Such claims can cause friction with your spouse; guilt-ridden, your partner could side with your stepkids and restrict or withhold things from your stepfamily, or simply hand them over to your stepkids without consulting you—the sewing machine could be shelved; the item from Dad's collection could be given to the children outright.

You will have to be understanding, realizing that your partner could be in the difficult position of pleasing no one —neither you nor your stepchildren. So before you and your mate either assume that something belongs in your new home or make plans to dispose of it, go over the objections in your household and determine what might interest your stepkids. Decide on a way to approach them about your plans for those items before an awkward situation develops. One possibility is to sit down and calmly discuss matters as a couple with your stepchildren and even give them a chance to take what has sentimental value for them.

Nothing is worth unnecessary hard feelings; respect your stepchildrens' positions if they are being reasonable. Hopefully, through foresight, you will avoid arguments and resolve matters peacefully. However, peace at any price isn't the answer, either. Never give in to manipulation—you could set a bad precedent, positioning yourself to be taken advantage of in the future.

You also need to plan for the day when one of you dies. Thus, you and your mate should discuss and determine the disposal of the assets you either have now, or plan to acquire, and redraw your wills to reflect your decisions. If you have or expect to have a great deal, you should probably consult an estate planning attorney.

In any case, you should think carefully about what you want to leave your partner, your stepkids, and your children, if you have any. Never assume that terms such as "family" and "children" are clearly defined and understood in a will. It may not adequately cover your actual "step-situation" and stepchildren. Check with a lawyer to make sure your will covers all the survivors you wish to include, especially if you and your partner are not married. If you die without any will at all, state law will govern the distribution of your estate. Generally, spouses get one-third to one-half, while children—not stepchildren—divide the rest.

You and your partner may want discuss your wills with with the rest of the family in order to get their opinions and to inform them in advance of your decisions. That will help avoid having your stepchildren get upset should they learn indirectly of significant changes in what they thought would be passed on to them. This can be a problem when older people remarry. Their children can grow fearful about how the new marriage will affect their inheritance.

If you are in a stepfamily where each adult has children, you may not want to leave your estate to your partner, because it can be used against your wishes to support your stepchildren instead of your birth children. Also, if your spouse remarries, a stranger may gain control of your assets.

Sometimes, parents set up trusts for their birth children to make sure they are provided for after the parents' deaths. If your partner is interested in taking that step, but the prospect makes you feel financially insecure, you may want to bring up the possibility that a trust can still be established without cutting you out of things altogether. For instance, there are arrangements such as "by-pass trusts" under which a surviving spouse, subject to some regulation, is beneficiary until his or her death, whereupon the estate transfers to the children. If your partner wants to set up a trust, you may want to discuss a bypass. Also, it is possible—and cheaper—to add a stipulation to a will for a "testamentary trust," a provision by which someone can specify which assets are for the children, and how and when they should receive them.

You may be wondering what to do about that major asset in the lives of many of us: a residence. One suggestion is that each new spouse contribute something towards the purchase to foster family unity and economic balance between the adults. Stepparents may also want to consider taking title as "tenants in common." That designation permits a more flexible distribution of each adult's share of the property after death.

When the parent in a stepfamily leaves property shares to his or her kids, trouble can begin to brew if the children want to sell and the stepparent does not. Can that situation be avoided? Yes. If your funds will be limited, your partner could take out an insurance policy that will pay you enough to buy out your stepchildren, if need be.

◆　　◆　　◆

Now it is time for you to turn to the income side of the ledger. Think broadly and use a lot of foresight, given recent unemployment figures. Is your source of employment stable? The loss of a job is one of the biggest crises a person can endure. If you lost yours, do you live in an area with a diverse economy that is conducive to relatively low unemployment? Do you have the education and training to shift careers if necessary? What are your chances for advancement? Will you need to spend money on school-ing in order to stay current and competitive in your field?

Another potential criis would be caused by illness. If your job pays your health insurance and you will be paying the health costs for stepchildren, does the policy cover stepchildren? Some plans do, but others don't. You should check and proceed accordingly. Also, if you or your partner lost your jobs, would you still have health insur-ance? If not, would you be able to afford it, or could you pay for your family's health care?

Will you be a dual income couple? Is each of you healthy enough to keep working and care for the children? Do both of you want to work? Should you? Good parent-ing involves a significant time investment, and stepfamilies can have a lot of stepchildren. Is it realistic and/or neces-sary that both adults be outside the home during the day? What are your partner's expectations? Your own?

Many birth mothers work so that they can support their families, but if you are a stepmom, without children, who has been in the workplace or on a career track, and you have acquired some hard-earned autonomy, you may be reluctant to give up your economic independence and stay home. Yet, as the woman, you may feel more pressure to make that choice. Your partner should be sensitive to your situation, respect your feelings, and not automatically expect you to be the one to change.

All in all, stepparents may have to reevaluate whether they want or need to continue putting in long hours at the office, or being away so much because of their jobs. While the demands of some jobs force people to travel or work long hours, and these people complain that their work limits their ability to parent, others use professional demands to avoid domestic responsibilities. Be honest about your behavior, and the reasons for it, and try to strike the best possible balance.

And what are you and your partner's views about your children holding down jobs while they are in school? Some educators worry that younger children, in particular, risk neglecting their studies when they combine school and work.

Set some parameters as you discuss these matters with your partner. How much and when should the kids work? What spending and savings rules apply to them? Do you expect your stepkids to contribute some of their earnings to the family? If you do, take the approach outlined for asking an adult stepchild to pay room and board.

BUDGETING

Once you and your partner have determined your expenses and have a pretty good idea about your income, you should develop a system for expenditures.

Be honest with yourselves and each other about your spending habits and those of your children. Try to reach a reasonable compromise where you diverge. You may want to think about setting an overall ceiling on your stepfamily that breaks down into limits on adults and children. Use ample foresight. If the kids' ages are spread out, you will have make sure you put aside enough money to cover caring for them over longer period of time.

One rule of thumb is to have your stepfamily cut its spending by at least five percent in order to beef up its savings. Reducing unnecessary purchases of clothing and entertainment expenses; shopping the classifieds, thrift stores, or yard sales; buying used cars instead of new; joining food clubs and shopping for generic brand items; refinancing; and turning to cheaper schools are some money savers.

However, it is probably wise not to eradicate all expenditures for amusement from your budget. You will probably want to put aside some money to do things as a family, and for you and your partner to have a respite from parenting.

You don't have to break the bank. The family can visit sites in your area, see an afternoon movie(when prices are reduced), or do something equally economical, like renting videos to watch together. Meanwhile, adults can escape to nearby towns for weekend getaways, or stay in-town, pay a babysitter, and spend a couple of hours out once in awhile. These outlets can be inexpensive as well as therapeutic.

In any event, when money has to be spent, who is going to be the one to act as banker? Is Bobby always going to hit up whomever happens to be home, or will there be a better organized, fairer way to meet everyday costs? Who doles out allowances? Writes the rent check? Pays the utilities? Whose wallet will thin when bills from family vacations drift in?

Answers may lie in "two pot" and "common pot" financial management. Under the former, you separate the assets and resources you had before your stepfamily formed. You take care of your own business, including obligations from the past such as alimony, child support and old mortgages, as well as present costs such as medical and clothing bills for yourselves and your kids, allowances for your children, housing and automobile expenses.

For those bills that apply to everyone in the stepfamily, you and your mate also set up and contribute equally (or fairly) to a kitty. It covers small, spur-of-the-moment miscellaneous expenses, as well as bigger costs such as those for household goods, furniture, groceries, utilities, insurance, and family recreation and entertainment.

Under this approach, Bobby's request could be met with funds from one of two places.Obviously, you would have to give money to Bobby, since he needs his twenty dollars right away, and no other adult is home. But if you have made a decision in advance,you could be reimbursed by your spouse because you both have agreed to pay for your own kids' educational expenses, or Bobby's money could come from the common kitty you and your partner set up. The key thing would be that there is a defined system for handling payouts and keeping people from being or feeling financially put upon or used. In addition, the two-pot system may be an ideal balance, especially in the delicate early stages of stepfamily life. It allows couples to preserve their financial autonomy, yet collaborate on some family expenses. However, you should guard against one major potential drawback—living as separate financial entities may prove a deterant to striving for complete stepfamily unity.

A second suggestion, the common pot approach, has the couple merge resources. This may seem riskier because extracting yourself from your relationship will be more difficult when you surrender your monetary independence and blend everything. Nevertheless, this streamlining can reduce chances for divisive discussions about who pays for what.

Furthermore, it can have great symbolic and emotional value. It signals that you and your partner are committed to your joint future, unlike the two-pot setup which encourages biological loyalties and personal autonomy. Under this financial arrangement, Bobby's request becomes a *family* expense—nothing more—and nothing less.

Of course, deciding upon these methods now assumes you and your partner did not enter into pre-nuptial agreement. A "pre-nup" spells out each partner's financial privileges and responsibilities, and specifies how assets will be divided in the event of a death or divorce. People enter prenuptual agreements so that the division of assets is agreed upon prior to marriage.

Typically, prenups require full disclosure of both parties' resources. As legally binding contracts, lawyers must execute them, thereby incurring legal fees. Pre-nups can give stepfamilies a businesslike chill, but they can also reduce tensions by reassuring the children of a former marriage that they will not be disinherited by a new union. In addition, some experts urge stepparents to insist on pre-nups so they know where they are going to stand legally with their stepchildren—whether or not their marriage succeeds—and to give themselves clear idea of where they will be financially with their spouse as they start out as a couple.

However, because property is automatically commingled in some states, couples who sign a pre-nuptial agreement are also advised to execute a "property status agreement." That document delineates ownership and specifies which assets can and cannot be claimed by a spouse. One last word on pre-nuptial agreements: if you go for one, make sure it reflects other documents, such as your will (or vice versa). Conflicting instructions among your personal planning papers could cause many unwanted complications.

In sum, the universal advice on money and stepparenthood is this: know what you are getting into and avoid situations where the handling of resources blocks unity. Financial dealings should unify your stepfamily in a sensible way that accommodates family and individual needs. They should not be used or have the affect of keeping your stepfamily divided.

Indeed, money is a sensitive area in many stepfamilies. Fortunately, you may not need to be so guarded once your relationship develops and matures, and everyone is more trusting. Until then, parents need to bear the daily "financial times" to their older children. They must lead by telling the children what their allowances are going to be, what they are expected to contribute to the household, what they will have to pay to cover their share of the auto insurance, whether they have to attend community college instead of their dream university and what their inheritance will be. That will save you from being the bearer of bad or serious news, or accused of interfering in a critical situation.

Lastly, while it is good to set up accounting systems, you shouldn't be too rigid or businesslike. Fairness and flexibility on the part of everyone—not iron-clad, impersonal emphasis on strict equality and accountability—is the better way to go. Bobby wants money? Ask yourself if his request is reasonable. If it is and you have money to spare, perhaps you should provide your stepson with what he needs and not worry. Giving from the heart, rather than any special account, could leave you much better off in the long run.

LEGAL ISSUES

Let's draw another scene to make you aware of an area that is frequently overlooked: stepparents and the law.

You bond with your stepson Bobby, who was ten when you became his stepparent. Over time, he matures and grows into a very likeable young man. Before long, you are looking upon him as the son you never had, while he calls you mom or dad and really means it.

Then, tragedy strikes. Your spouse becomes ill and dies. Luckily, because of you and your mate's estate planning, you will be able to stay in the house you both shared. But one of the things that helps make any house a home—

loving children—is not something you can legally claim. Like virtually all stepparents, you have a lot of responsibilities, but very few rights. In this particular instance, you probably have no right to Bobby.

As a minor, he is taken in by the non-custodial parent, or some other blood relative, even though he still has a home with you—and he feels attached. in Bobby's case, hehas to leave and becomes upset the day he learns he is no longer going to be able to live with you. You don't think you'll ever be able to shake the memory of how he slammed his bedroom door and cried.

Ultimately, you are left shattered twice over; you have not only lost your partner, but you have also been forced to say goodbye to the boy whom you regard as your own by a most important unit of measure: your heart.

An even likelier variation? You and Bobby bond, but you and your spouse don't. You divorce, split by the same pressures that cause remarriages to fail at high rates. Although today, in a few court caes, stepparents have been granted visiting rights, most likelyyou have no rights to Bobby, even though you have been a devoted parent. The situation is hard on you both. "Neither biology nor law gave me the right to claim such a role," a stepfather reported once. He was writing about how he reacted when hi sstep child insisted on calling him dad after the author and the child's mother split up.He first met his stepson when the boy was an eighteen-month-old "tiny little body topped off by a big head covered with blond hair." Years later, with wrenching concern, the stepkid asked his former stepdad, "Don't you want to be my father anymore?"

Situations like these may not be part of your expectations right now. But they happen, and knowing where you stand legally as a stepparent from the start will help you avoid being victimized, a hidden casualty of circumstances that may not directly involve you.

While legal conditions may change for the better as more and more stepfathers and stepmothers take parenting roles all over the world, stepparents are basically invisible in the eyes of the law.

In the United States, for example, states generally determine their responsibilities and rights. Nonetheless, you can not delay being wise legally; check with a family law attorney, or your area's legal associations for current, specific and complete information that applies.

Could you have adopted Bobby as the solution to everything? Maybe. Certainly, adoption is the one clear way for stepparents to gain rights towards their stepchildren. But it isn't always possible, or the answer in the cases of divorce as well as foster parenting, etc.

Certain conditions must exist first. The birth parent must either be dead, lose rights to the child for egregious reasons such as abandonment, or give consent. (But bear in mind that your stepchild could lose his inheritance, when the parent agrees to the adoption.)

Even with legal clearance, however, adoption is not always a good choice with stepchildren of a remarriage or after a parrent's death. Much depends on the age and circumstances of your stepchild. Generally, the younger the better seems to be one rule that governs the chances for an adopted child to have close ties with an unrelated adult. But with a very young age comes an issue. In all likelihood, the child will not remember anything, so you will have to weigh whether and how you are going to bring up the adoption. The wisest course would be for you to consult with a professional counselor first for the best tips on to how to break the news to your stepchild.

But you have to be careful no matter what the situation is. Examine your motives and respect the feelings of your stepson or stepdaughter. Sometimes, well-meaning people delude themselves that adoption cements fragile relationships with stepchildren. There is no guarantee it does, especially if it is a forced substitute for a stepparent-stepchild bond. Nothing takes the place of that. If you and your stepchild have a good relationship, adoption could be of marginal benefit. If yours is bad, it won't be able to help.

Remember, too, that you don't face an "all-or-nothing" proposition. You can be central in your stepchild's life, and your stepchild can even come to use your name, or change over to it legally without an adoption taking place. Such moves can be a compromise when a caring outside parent is involved who, on one hand, wonders whether a child should be adopted to help the kid adjust, but on the other, balks at giving up parental rights.

With respect to custody matters, you may want to look into having visitation rights made part of a pre-nuptial agreement. Relatively few states give stepparents the right to sue for visitation to stepchildren. Even if your spouse names you guardian in a will, parents and blood relatives may have the edge in custodial claims.

But you can defend against that by having your partner set up a trust for his or her children and name you as a trustee. That would accomplish two things: your spouse would manage to keep his or her estate away from his or her ex, and you would have a clear and justifiable reason for staying involved with your stepkids.

There is a flip side. If you have few legal rights, it is also true that you have few legal obligations. Generally, stepparents are not legally required to support or be responsible for their stepchildren. Your stepchildren are free to use your surname, but unless you adopt, it is not a legal name.

Moreover, your stepkids must be named in your will to have a right to your estate; otherwise, a blood relative's claim takes precedence.

Think twice, though, if you believe your invisibility in the eyes of the law exempts you completely from any legal involvement with your stepchildren. In some states, if you promise to support your stepkids, and your spouse gets to the point of relying on you, you can be held liable for child support if you divorce. One attorney goes so far as to say, "There is a danger in being very nice," he says. "You could be hit" by the court—forced, in other words, to continue in your role as supporter.

Also, your finances, personal life, and even your parenting may come under scrutiny. If you and your partner do not have a prenuptial agreement, and you do not keep your respective resources separate, you could be asked about your income and financial obligations during review hearings on alimony or child support which involve your partner and his or her former spouse.

In such cases, a common rationale is that the arrival of the stepparent takes financial pressure off the parent and, in effect, frees him or her to be more supportive.

Some stepparents feel invaded and resent being dragged into legal affairs which do not concern them directly. They find it hard to accept being put under detailed examination and having their resources linked with their spouses'. And if one adult's financial obligations are increased, everyone in a new stepfamily suffers by having to live with that loss of income. This practice amounts to wrongful seizure of property, some advocates argue. Their point—the stepparent is not party to the parent's divorce agreement.

You can feel violated other ways, too. In custody fights involving your partner and his or her former spouse, your fitness as a parent may come under scrutiny. Your relationship with your stepchild may be examined by mental health experts, or the ex may raise questions about your sexual attitudes and behavior, discipline techniques, and parenting generally. Some stepparents have felt violated after their partners' former spouses publically misconstrued their well-intentioned actions. As divorce attorney Dee Samuels puts it: "A stepchild may complain to the out-of-home parent, and then the court is there to second guess you."

Lastly, a couple of other areas should be mentioned as potential legal pitfalls. As a stepparent, you may be unable to authorize emergency medical treatment for your stepchildren at a hospital. To avoid that, encourage the parents of your stepkids to fill out a limited power of attorney that gives you that right.

And be aware that medical emergencies are not the only situations in which you may be blocked. For instance, in one case, a stepparent was not allowed to pick up his stepchild at an airport when authorities learned that their last names differed. The snag was probably frustrating and inconvenient for everyone, but insulting and demoralizing for the stepparent in particular. To spare yourself, anticipate. In family situations where you have no authority, have your partner get your stepchild, or contact authorities beforehand and determine whether and what authorization is required.

Also, as the stepparent, you may be stopped from picking your stepchild up at school, or trying to get his or her school records. Generally, you can't expect education officials to treat you as a parent unless you make it a point to let them know who you are. Authorities may be guarded because they fear releasing children to undesirables such as irresponsible non-custodial parents who could kidnap kids or harm them some other way.

How can you break the ice with your stepchild's school? Assuming you discuss things first with your partner and stepchildren, the two of you may want to write the principal, teachers, and guidance counselor explaining who you are and asking for a meeting with them. The letter will be a clear means of introduction and serve as a tangible record of your status.

At the meeting, have your partner endorse your involvement. When it is your turn to talk, show them that you are a caring parent. Tell them you are interested in your stepchild's education; you want to be notified about school events and activities, especially parent-teacher conferences; and you are among the persons who can be contacted when discipline problems and emergencies arise. You may also want to give your perspective on how early stepfamily life is affecting your stepchild. Be honest. If family members are having a rough time adjusting, it may help school officials to know that in order to have more insight towards students.

There will be other benefits, too. Frequently, educators put children in the position of notifying adults about school matters. That can be awkward and confusing for stepkids, however. If one adult is someone new in their life, a child may be unsure about saying anything. By coming forward, you will preclude your stepchild from having those unsettling feelings. You can also take initiative by obtaining a school calendar and using it to keep abreast of important developments throughout the year.

Your involvement should at least make you *feel* less like an outsider in your stepfamily, though your spouse should take the lead dealing with your stepson's or stepdaughter's educators. You may be surprised by the reception you receive, too. These days, education can be a pretty grim business as schools have become settings for all sorts of social ills. Teachers welcome and *need* support from interested and committed adults, step-parents and parents alike.

Most of all, your involvement should demonstrate clearly to your stepchildren that you care and are going to be concerned when they stumble, proud when they achieve.

Part Two...
Stepfatherhood

Some of the factors which determine how you will do as a stepfather are:
- the age, gender, and temperament of your stepkids
- your own temperament, circumstances and attitudes
- your mutual marital communication and devotion
- the involvement of your stepchildrens' birth father

Stepfatherhood is relatively smooth for many men. They and their stepkids fit together well, other conditions which bear on stepfamilies are helpful, and everyone knows some happiness and fulfillment. The findings of researcher Nicholas Zill, as reported in an essay included in *Impact of Divorce, Single Parenting, and Stepparenting on Children*, a book edited by E. Mavis Hetherington and Josephine Arasteh, actually seem to indicate that the addition of a stepfather to a "mother-only family usually produces a net gain for the family because it improves the family's financial condition without making the children's psychological well-being worse."

But there are pitfalls. For example, early on, you may find that very little can match or penetrate the history and blood lines connecting your stepchildren to their mother *and* father. Chances are "Where have *you* been?" will be written on your stepchildren's faces when you try to give them advice. It will take time for you to acquire any paternal authority.

Because you have no biological bond to them, your stepkids may want to know what right you have to correct them about anything. "I have (or *had*) a father, thank you!" could be their attitude. Emboldened because they and mom endured alone, before you ever showed up, they could feel that they don't need you to tell them what to drive, when to be home, or how to behave. Or they may just not be responsive. Stepfathers who think they are a knight on a rescue mission could quickly eat humble pie should they meet up with stepkids who take care of themselves and act independently.

You could have other problems as well. Sometimes, mothers interfere, making life more difficult for stepfathers. Typically, this happens when partners of stepparents feel guilty about their kids' post-divorce life; they don't want to see them picked-on. Or your partner may feel insecure about having her children get close to someone new because she doesn't want them to get hurt again, or to see their loyalties divided. Until now, her kids may have been her security blanket, so she is overprotective.

And even if they like you, your stepchildren may not act as though they do. They could make you think that in their eyes you are nothing short of Attila the Hun. "If we show interest or caring towards our stepdad," they may wonder, "Will that mean I am being disloyal to my own father? Who is really in charge of my life? Who should I invite to my school activities or sporting events? What if my dad tells me to do one thing—but my stepfather tells me to do another? Who do I listen to?" Frustrated, your stepchildren may be downright nasty when you are around. It may be the best way they know of to keep their loyalty to dad intact.

Of course, there are also stepkids who try to subvert a couple's attempt to build a new stepfamily. They could want their birth father back while you seem to stand right in the way of this goal, or they could be jealous of sharing their time with mom. If you think you are immune to such challenges, think again.

One "star" of the world of stepfathers—the esteemed child expert Dr. Benjamin Spock—had his problems when he became a father figure for an eleven-year-old step-daughter. His biggest mistake, as the esteemed doctor recalls in a *Redbook* article, was being too critical. Spock took issue with everything, from his stepchild's unwilling-ness to spend time with him and his wife, to her refusal to wear corrective dental headgear. He exploded several times. Once, Spock told his stepdaughter she was the rudest person he had ever met!

Like other stepfathers, Spock endured the consequences of getting in the middle of a tight mother-child bond. His stepdaughter had a very close relationship with her mother for many years. Suddenly, though, she was seeing her only five months of the year, as her mom now travelled exten-sively with her new husband. The change seemed instan-taneous, was intrusive and upsetting, and triggered strong feelings of insecurity. The girl had only met Spock once before he married her mother. She never really knew him, and what little she could determine did not look promising, either. Her stepdad was sixty years older, far removed from the values, interests, and tastes of her young world. Yet, Spock was also a renowned authority on children. If he could have difficulty, so can you.

Discipline

Some mothers may still expect their spouses to become the primary disciplinarians after marriage. This can cause a stepfather some serious trouble. Many stepfathers founder because they can't overcome their partners' greater influence over the children, or their stepchildrens' lack of built-in respect for them. Still, they plough ahead haplessly, designated disciplinarians, pressured by mates, dated societal expectations, their own needs or some of each.

They raise their voices. They become proverbial bulls in the china shops of their stepchildrens' fragile psyches. Quick to punish, they view every infraction in black and white terms and as personal affronts. Possibly, they spank or engage in or provoke physical confrontations. Overall, they expect their stepchildren to respond to their "hard chagrin'" stepparenting. In these stepdads' minds, they are knights rescuing stressed-out partners from the strain of single parenthood.

Here is another possible stepparenting scenario—this one involves a stepfather disciplining an older child:

It is a weekend night. You walk in as a conversation is concluding between Grace, your new stepdaughter, and your partner.

"Why is Grace in such a hurry?" you wonder, watching her leap up from the table. You keep quiet, but it isn't easy. You wince as Grace throws open the refrigerator door, unscrews a juice container, stops talking momentarily, gulps the juice down, then resumes chattering away as she aimlessly screws the lid back on.

A voice goes off in your head: "Why doesn't her mother *say* something?"

Your wife does reproach Grace, but the scold sounds more like a plea than a reprimand. It is obvious to you that this kid has not had the tough kind of discipline she needs.

As you take in more of the scene, your mood darkens as your feelings of being ineffectual and left out rise up. Soon, you are so negative you are willing to bet Grace has juice on her hands and has made the handle on the refrigerator door sticky again.

Anyway, you decide to park yourself in a living room chair. You have been around Grace enough by now to know that she likes to primp in the hall mirror. That stop is not far from where you are sitting.

You want a last chance to ask her some questions before she goes out. As Grace's stepfather, you feel *some* duty to know *something* about what is going on, and where she is headed.

Almost on cue, Grace arrives, plants herself and begins to touch up her hair. That done, she turns to head out, coming right toward you. You remind yourself that Grace plans to use the family car.

"Where are you going?"

You try to be forceful, yet not too stern, but it doesn't work. You sound like a cop.

"Out," Grace says, turning around distractedly to look in the mirror one last time. And then she takes off.

Mildly disgruntled, you drift back to the kitchen. The fridge handle *is* dirty. You reach in and dump out the juice. So much for saving on groceries . . . but it is that handle you are mulling over hours later as you toss and turn, and stare at the clock on the bedstand.

It's 1:00 A.M. Where is Grace? Where is the car? Now, the disciplinarian-stepfather who would try to get Grace to "shape up" tosses in his bed, mumbling grumpy words, such as:

"Just who does Grace think she is? I saw the look in her eye when she went by me as she headed out the door. Proud—she *loved* showing me up. She doesn't respect me as a father. She senses I don't like her driving around so late, but she *insists* on doing that anyway.

"Well, this is the last time *that* is ever going to happen. If Grace wants to drive somebody's car, let her drive her father's. She can no longer have ours—I don't care if it means she has to quit her part-time job or stop participating in school activities

"Stepfather or not, I'm still the man of the house, and I'll set the rules if no one else will—my wife sure doesn't seem to be in control.

"What the heck has she been doing all these years?

"No wonder Grace is a brat."

There are also stepfathers who are unnerved by the tight mother-child bond. They retreat rather than charge. Feeling like unwanted relatives who have overstayed a welcome, these stepdads become put off and insecure because they don't seem to inspire respect or easy communication. Their thoughts echo that famous Rodney Dangerfield cry of self-pity, "I don't get no respect!"

Miffed, suffering from a loss of face, resentful, they wash their hands of parenting and pull back. They leave everything to their partners, telling themselves they formed their union to be with them, not the stepkids.

The stepfather who tosses and turns, wanting to wash his hands of Grace *and* stepparenting, thinks like this:

"You are foolish to get upset. You are the *step*father, remember? There is no reason to be so involved. You have a big week at work ahead of you. Go to sleep already. Why trouble yourself? You don't seem to be taken very seriously. You'll never crack that exclusive mother-daughter chitchat that is constantly going on between your wife and Grace. When you come around, they look at you like you're an alien from another galaxy. When are you finally going to wise up and grow tired of being cut out?

"You should just withdraw. Grace is not worth the bother and she is not your responsibility, plain and simple—

let her *father* deal with her. Your life will be much easier, and you won't find yourself having any more sleepless nights.

"Besides, you have much better things to do than worry about some silly teenager whose priorities are boys, the telephone and the car, in no particular order."

So how do you keep from being the unrealistic disciplinarian or the remote and detached observer? Your goal should be to strike a balance. You do not want to bowl over your stepchildren—and you should not to be bowled over *by* them, either.

In interviews and publications such as *Current Health*, stepparents, therapists and other experts have indicated that the pre- and early teen years are when most of the trouble hits. If you are a stepfather to children in that age range, therefore, it may be best not to try to shape or control your stepchildren's behavior, but to simply support your partner's actions instead. Try to be warm, approachable, responsive and open. You should be honest about your expectations and keep them reasonable, and you should not excuse yourself from anything. You are the stepparent John Leonard was referring to in his 1984 *Harper's Bazaar* article, "Second Marriage—First Class Romance," when he wrote, "I can no longer *demand* the affection or the respect of my wife or my children. Like John Houseman, I must *earn* it."

You have a say in what goes on at home, but your opinions and actions as to your stepchildren should be discriminating and controlled. They are neither overbearing nor intrusive. You do not demand obedience, and you are slow to anger and criticism. You are a good friend, a listener, a caring and interested adult. Simply, you are *there*.

People who have written fondly of stepfathers tell of men who gamely went along, even enjoyed, step children's pranks and horseplay; were given to bringing home small but thoughtful gifts that expressed how much they cared; gave children a chance to speak and encouraged them to sort out their problems for themselves with the benefit of a mildly expressed adult perspective; and treated them as if they had something on the ball. Usually, these stepfathers did what they did with no clear idea of what reward, if any, they would get. But over the long run, as evidenced by their stepchildren's stories, they harvested great appreciation, even love.

Think of the uncle whom you liked and respected, who always took a friendly, unthreatening interest in your life—the person whom you could count on to lend an ear, crack a joke or just be calmly accepting, no questions asked. Imitate him.

THE WAY TO THE MIDDLE

You now understand *what* you have to do. Going to extremes is out; being moderate is in. But *how* do you manage to do that?

Set your fuse on a slow burn. Men, more than women, may have the hardest time saving face in the presence of back talking stepkids. As stepfather, the biggest temptation in the world may be to become confrontational—to strike back with a shouted retort, a demand, a stinging remark, or a declared punishment. You may find yourself bellowing orders like, "You will go up to your room *now* and not come down until *I* tell you!"—especially when dealing with a stepchild who is critical, nasty or just trying to goad you with obnoxious behavior. Being drawn into an argument is only going to lead to hard feelings and delay having a trusting, enjoyable relationship.

A good example would be if your stepchild, upon being told that he has turn off the TV and go to bed, yells, "You're always telling me what to do! Or it's 'don't do this' and 'don't do that'—I'm tired of it!" The stepfather who is headed for more trouble might respond: "You're going to bed because I'm telling you to!"

The thin-skinned stepdad—the one who's quick to withdraw in the face of stepparenthood's challenges—may hear the shrill accusation and say to himself, "This is the last time I ever worry about when this kid goes to bed. Let his mother tell him next time. I couldn't care less if he's too sleepy tomorrow to be much good in school."

Instead, you would be better off mustering an even voice and simply repeating that it is time for the child to go to bed. Perhaps he or she will just be testing, deciding to leave well enough alone once it is clear that you are keeping cool and are not going to be drawn into a shouting match.

Another tactic might be to respond with a calm, rational explanation of why your stepchild's criticism is not justified: it has been made clear to him that bedtime is 9:30; that is one of the house rules all the children live by so the household can function well and fairly for all.

Perhaps, too, you could calmly ask your stepson if he thinks you're against him. As he answers, gently remind him of times when you have defended him in front of mom —say, that instance the previous week when you advocated that he be able to stay up a little late to watch the conclusion of a game. If you did that, you might ask, how could he say that you are always telling him what to do. In other words, help him see your even-handedness.

Have your mate help enforce the rules. It is unavoidable that stepparents are going to be in situations where they have to discipline, but it is always better in the early stage of stepfamily life to have the rules articulated by the biological parent—especially when one comes under serious challenge from kids.

Lastly, if you *are* always telling your stepkids what to do, stop. It will undermine your authority when there is a legitimate reason to bring it to bear. If you are being reasonable with your stepchildren most of the time, they will have less reason to rebel and less evidence to support their cause when they start to criticize you.

Overall, you can help ease matters with your stepchildren with a good talk. Reassure them by saying several things:

- ◆ their confusion about loyalties is normal, given the very nature of stepfamily life
- ◆ you do not intend to replace their dad—their relationship with him cannot be duplicated; it is important and you respect it.
- ◆ you want to work on building a unique and mutually satisfying friendship
- ◆ you have tried not to come into their lives with rigid expectations, but you do expect to be treated with the respect due an "authoritative" parent

Try to engage your stepchildren, but you do not have to think grandly, or go to great lengths to try to impress them. For all of your good intentions, little may seem to register with them if for no other reason that many kids, teenagers especially, are not that communicative. In a *New York Times* article titled "Stepfathers: the Shoes RarelyFit,"writer Jon Nordheimer reported one disgruntled stepfather saying, "Let's go camping this weekend, let's go to a movie, let's play monopoly, I tell them. But all I get are these drop-dead looks and they go running off to their father's house and tell him I pick my teeth after dinner or that my own kids who visit us on weekends are dorks."

By trying you will have done your part, and in its own way, the message of your good intentions may get through. Determine your stepkids' interests and be content with inviting them along for a mild level of activity at first. Increase your outreach gradually as you get a response, and keep cool throughout. One of the myths of stepfamily life is that the whole family must do things together. Not so. Respect your partner's time with the kids; let as much as possible of what went on before you joined the family continue, and do not allow yourself to feel threatened. Rather, start to establish your own relationship with your stepchildren.

HAVE GOOD COUPLE COMMUNICATION

On their own, some stepfathers go to extremes and then crash or get turned off to stepparenthood despite pleas and talks from their partners. But some are set up for those eventualities by their partners. These are women who seek male figures to get their children in line. As single parents, they are weary of always playing the role of "policeman." Misguidedly, they sometimes think a stepfather is literally the man for the job. In stepfamilies, as in other families however, discipline is a two-person job and good couple communication is very important.

In the preceding anecdote about Grace, it is implicit that communication between the adults is virtually nil. Had it been otherwise, the stepfather might not have had his extreme thoughts, and his parenting technique would have been much more subtle. In a private session with his partner he should have expressed his concern that driving around at night is much more unsafe than it used to be, especially for a woman. He may have heard in response that Grace cannot be kept "caged up," because she might rebel completely that way, or that she was only headed a short distance and planned to call when she got there and would be out with a couple of level-headed friends.

He should also have used time alone with his wife to vent his feelings about the family car being used inappropriately or about the lateness of Grace's curfew. He may then have been reminded that Grace is a safe driver and is at the age where she has to be given some freedoms, provided she does not abuse them.

A discussion must take place between adults who respect, support, listen to and compromise with each other.

They can then relay their decision through the one with the best odds of penetrating teenage obstinacy.

DON'T TRY TO REPLACE DAD

As you have probably guessed by now that conditions are not ripe for you and your stepchildrens' father to be best buddies. Jealousies and disputes between stepdads and dads are normal, but they don't have to be hostile. Problems between stepfathers and fathers tend to diminish with time, and many stepdads consider them to be of minor concern. However, differences can become more pronounced when no attempt is made to resolve them, so stay open-minded and accepting on this score and be as honest as possible with yourself.

If you feel insecure over the father in your stepchildrens' lives, this could reflect your own outsider status in your new stepfamily as much as anything else. Recognize that, and be assured that time will settle most problems of this nature.

Whatever you do, avoid falling into the funk of thinking you will never mean anything to your stepchildren. According to a recent report in *Psychology Today*, research by psychologist John Santrock, children raised by stepfathers—young boys, especially—do very well and sometimes even better than kids raised in single-parent households. Much depends, however, on the level of involvement desired by the father of your stepchildren.

If your stepkids are close with their dad, you may not need to be a father to them, or even have much opportunity to be so. But if the opposite is true, they may be more open to having an adult male caretaker and protector.

Generally, young children with a great dependency on adults may quickly accept a stepfather's help and discipline. But acceptance drops off the higher up in age you go. Usually, teenagers are trying to break from all adult authority. They adhere to parental rule only out of fear, love and respect. As a stepfather, you may never have claim to any of that. With older stepchildren, you have to be ready for just about anything, from being ignored to being punched. The case of Jim dramatically illustrates this point.

Concerned because his eighteen-year-old stepson was a failing student, Jim decided to meet with the boy's father to urge him to actively encourage his son. However, when the boy heard that the men had talked, he felt that Jim had interfered. Even though his father had a long history of parental neglect, the meeting made him so mad he went home, confronted Jim in an ugly scene and socked him.

According to Jim and his wife Mary, this physical blow was the closing shot in a long period in which the boy had been living at home, frustrated and acting difficult. After the incident, the boy moved into a nearby apartment, bankrolled by the couple. Jim and Mary cite the negligence of the father as the reason for the teenager's troubles. They add that it probably angered the stepson to see Jim being devoted to his own children.

How does Jim feel now? Though still smarting from the punch, he tries to be fair about it.

"It's a tense, tough, situation," Jim says, with just a trace of resentment. I love and care for my wife. I would have been long gone if I didn't."

Should Jim have gone to see the father?

There are probably thousands of situations, most of them far less dramatic, where stepfathers ask themselves this very question. At best, the answer is a general one: it's always good for adults to get along and cooperate on parenting. Assuming Jim went over to get the father's input, he did the right thing, though it would appear that he might have been dreaming if the father had indeed been so neglectful all along.

As a stepfather, you are going to have to judge such situations for yourself. The bottom line is always to work on building cooperation and trust between parents and stepparents rather than resorting to criticism, making trouble or attempts to replace the father figure in your stepchildren's lives.

In Frank F. Fursterberg's article, "Child Care After Divorce and Remarriage," he reveals that a stepdad is not going to have his parenting compromised if his stepchild is in touch with the father. So even though your stepkids spend time with their dad and talk about him incessantly, you need not interpret this as slamming the door shut on you. You should just keep reminding yourself that you have something to offer your stepkids, and that it is there for them to take advantage of when they are ready.

Until then, if a "two-father" arrangement pertains in your situation, and seems to be working satisfactorily, keep at it.

Don't Wallow in Guilt—Act

Some stepdads who are also non-custodial parents feel guilty about having a relationship with stepchildren since they are not spending time with their own kids. Typically, they enter an emotional limbo, cut-off from all children until they can sort through their feelings and determine their priorities.

In some of the worst cases, stepfathers play kids off one another or size them up against each other. They think: my daughter is a better student than my stepdaughter, or my son is a better athlete than my stepson, or my adult step-daughter takes more interest in my health and needs that my real daughter ever did!

It will help if you can remember a couple of points. First, tell yourself that the past has passed and you are going to build on today and tomorrow. Your conscience should be clear if you can honestly say you are making reasonable attempts to meet all of your paternal obligations as you move forward.

Secondly, in these types of situations, you must see that much of the conflict lies with you, not your stepchildren or children. If you can admit that, you will be less quick to get upset and take out your frustrations on them. If you cannot, you risk ignoring the uniqueness of each of the children in your life and being insensitive to their real needs. Ultimately, the consequences can be very serious.

Bob, a former stepfather, failed to hit it off with his teenage stepson, a factor which contributed to the dissolution of his marriage. The boy was troubled other ways, but it was not helped by Bob and his former wife never having told him they planned to get married.

"He resented that," Bob says. "It came out in our fights."

Bob had gone to some trouble with his *own* kids, too. He says he spent time coaching them, reassuring them that he would still be their daddy and reminding them to respect their new stepmother. So why did Bob's wife fail to do a similar thing with her son?

"She was afraid of a confrontation," Bob says, implying that he was an accomplice to her denial of reality.

Ideally, the boy should have been informed by his mother of the impending marriage well beforehand. But Bob could have been more active in making sure she did. By being a party to the denial, staying completely out of things, and letting the huge surprise of the couple's marriage hit the boy full force, Bob helped himself to be seen as a villain in his stepson's eyes. He saw the need for his own kids to be forewarned; he should have extended the same consideration to his stepson.

The kid may still not have liked what he heard. He may still have yelled and screamed. At least he would have been dealing with the truth, however, which is a good thing for stepparents, and all other parents, to employ.

✦　　✦　　✦

So how do you know if you're on the road to being an "ideal" stepdad?

You display the following characteristics:

Moderation in your approach to stepkids—You do not barge into their lives as a disciplinarian, nor do you withdraw totally should you feel like an outsider; you aim for being involved, though a bit removed.

Realistic expectations—You realize that you will have little paternal standing at first, and accept having your partner lead in parenting your stepchildren; strive for any number of roles beyond that of traditional parent—fashioning yourself as an adult friend or kindly uncle are two possible approaches.

Patience—You work gradually at developing your relationship with your stepkids, rather than trying to compete with your partner's ex, your partner, or anyone else.

Unity in parenting—You maintain close communication with your mate about your stepchildren and you are mutually supportive.

Fairness—A balanced view of your past and appreciation for your stepchildrens' (and childrens') respective needs.

YOUR STEPCHILDREN'S BEHAVIOR IS FRIENDLY— BUT INAPPROPRIATE

Psychologist James Bray reported in a recent *Psychology Today* article that even when stepfathers do their best with stepchildren, progress usually comes only inch by inch. In some cases, young teens rebelled anew if their stepdads did their duty and held back from asserting themselves right away. That may sound depressing, but it is also the truth; you must be prepared to hang in there anyway, even though things stand a chance of being imperfect.

Some things will be out of your hands. Boys are more likely to have overnight visits with their fathers and, if they are eleven or older, may be living with their birth fathers. Because of this state of affairs, prepare to tamp down whatever paternal pride or yearnings you may have with respect to your stepsons. The claims you think you have on them could very well run aground in the wake of repeated visits to "dad's house."

However, pre-teen and teenage girls are often considered the bigger challenge for stepfathers. Usually, girls give their mothers more post-divorce support than do boys. Thus, stepfathers must often tread more lightly when it comes to parenting stepdaughters.

"I started disciplining too quickly," one stepfather named Neil says, recalling how he eventually forsook an authoritarian role with his teenage stepdaughter, a spoiled

girl whose mother had a history of being a poor disciplinarian who had been openly thwarted by the girl's father.
There was improvement in the child's attitude after Neil
and his wife were advised by a counselor to let the girl's
mother discipline, despite what had occurred before.
Unfortunately, the child's birth father and stepmother under-
mined the birth mother and stepfather's fresh start, and
the girl still refused to behave.

Neil's advice to stepfathers? Practice "maturity and
self-control," he says, "and seek help from support groups
such as the Stepfamily Association of America." (If it is any
consolation to you as a stepfather, Neil has had smooth sail-
ing with the girl's sister, who was five when he entered
her life. He describes his teenage daughter as having been
rebellious, but he implies that the younger girl was open to
him being a "father figure" from the start.)

Of course, Neil's situation could just as easily have
arisen if he were stepparenting a difficult stepson. So what
actions on your part *can* produce successful stepfather-
stepchild relationships? Lots and lots of verbal praise,
instead of policing your stepchildren by ever being on the
watch for a mistake, is often the best a stepdad can do. Make
it a point to compliment them when they do something
right around the house or achieve a goal at school.

However, although it is important to note that stepchildren sometimes act more congenial towards stepfathers
when they receive some *verbal* signs of affection from
them, *physical* gestures are another story. Both boys and
girls complain about being made uncomfortable by hugging or other forms of touching, even when there is no question that the stepfathers' motives are pure. Misinterpretation
of motive is more often a problem for stepfathers than stepmothers because, in many societies today, there is no
accepted way for men to express normal affection towards

a child unrelated to them. (This is not to say, however, that some abuse of stepchildren does not take place at the hands of stepparents of both sexes. Unfortunately, it does.)

It is also important to remember that time often proves to be a great healer, as the saying goes. You must be patient, wait things out and hope for the best. In Dr. Spock's case, mentioned previously, his stepdaughter was twenty years old before he wrote that "[we] are good friends most of the time." Looking back, he saw three or four years of rocky relations between them, then a pattern of four or five years of "gradual improvement. His stepdaughter concurred, saying that relations with "Ben" had become much better over the years. What finally made her realize that he cared about her? Spock sided with her in a disagreement she had with her mother over a particular issue that was very important to her.

But what is considered the norm—a stepchild resentful of a new adult man squarely in his or her life—may not necessarily be our fate as a stepparent. Sometimes, stepfathers encounter another side—teenage and even near-adult stepchildren who behave in friendly but nonetheless inappropriate ways, or who act negatively precisely because they are *jealous* of their new dads.

An example of the former situation would be if your stepdaughter bathes you with flattery and engages constantly in behavior to draw your attention. Some of this could be nothing but adolescent testing. Your stepdaughter may be starting to blossom into a woman, and she could just be trying out her charms on one of the men closest to her. However, provocative or overly ingratiating actions by a stepchild can also be a form of retaliation.

For example, your stepson could be trying to break free of mom's rule, shining up to you in the hope that you will lead him to freedom. Or, a stepdaughter may be angry about being displaced as her mother's sole confidant by the new husband, so she acts this way to get a rise out of her mother. (These types of situations apply to stepmothers and stepsons, as well.) If you have had teenagers before, you may be immune to these ploys. If you have not, you could be duped into some not-so-great stepfathering.

One solution is to clear the air with an honest family talk. You and your spouse should focus on the perception of yourselves as a single unit, and *you* should make it clear to all that you love and support your wife because of who she is and because you think she is acting in your stepchildren's best interests. In many cases, saying such things seriously and sincerely will be enough to make any stepchild back off.

You need not worry that being openly disapproving so early on will destroy your chances of ever being liked by your stepchildren, however. A stepchild's inappropriate behavior should not stop you from acting correctly as a stepfather. In the end, much time must pass and much mutual testing be endured before you are allotted your space in the "great hall" of stepdads.

PART THREE...
STEPMOTHERHOOD

You came into my life when it was upside down.
You encouraged me affectionately—
you turned my life around.
Sometimes, you differ with me,
but that's what stepmoms do.
So I'm writing this poem to say,
"Happy Birthday to you!"

This poem is part of the good news about stepmotherhood. Bonnie, a stepmom, received it from her grateful stepson. What made the child so appreciative? His own mother had taken no interest in him, and he was glad someone had finally ended years of neglect.

"I didn't do anything extraordinary," Bonnie says, playing down the caregiving she provided. "My stepson had been shown little love, and he was very confused."

But Bonnie *did* do a lot. Among other things, she helped reverse her stepson's poor school performance by having him diagnosed for debilitating medical conditions. This proved the right move. Doctors discovered that a chemical imbalance was affecting the boy's attention span. His grades improved following treatment.

"If that hadn't been found, I can't imagine what his self-esteem would be like today," Bonnie says.

Apparently, the discovery had little chance of happening any earlier through the efforts of the boy's mother.

According to Bonnie, her stepson's mom is the type who "sleeps 'til noon." She lives nearby, but remains completely uninvolved in her childrens' lives.

Meanwhile, Andy, a dad, holds a place next to Bonnie's stepson in the line of people grateful to stepmothers. He believes his second wife coaxed him into having a more realistic view of his two kids, and doing a better job of parenting overall.

"We were too wrapped up in each other," he says about his previous relationship with his children. He implies that their closeness verged on being shut off to others' views and lives, noting "we were too ingrown."

"A stepmother's influence is underrated," Andy declares. "She can offer an objective viewpoint which puts a family on a healthier course."

Dennis, another father, speaks well of his second wife's parenting, too. She got handed no small task. After years of separation and silence, Dennis' first wife suddenly sent the couple's son to live with his father. A teenager by then, the boy was a "juvenile delinquent," and his arrival was very upsetting.

"We were middle-aged, and we had our own hassles," Dennis remembers. "We were going crazy." His wife interpreted the boy's precipitous arrival "as an act of aggression on my first wife's part. He was dumped on us at a point when our lives were just starting to get pretty nice," Dennis explains. "It was like 'Here—take this!'""

Nevertheless, Dennis' spouse overcame her sense of victimization and tried to help.

"She would lose her cool and shout," he says, "but at the same time, she invested a lot. She would sit down with my son and talk with him, while I couldn't. "And he would open up to her like she was his therapist."

NEW EXPECTATIONS

The stories of people like Bonnie, Andy and Dennis, are encouraging but realtively rare. New stepmothers should get a boost from them, but they should not be deluded, either.

The plain truth is that stepmotherhood is considered the toughest role in stepfamily life. More than any other, it sits under the sharp focus of an unforgiving social microscope. As a rule, we eye stepmothers very skeptically; we just don't believe they can ever replace Mom, the idealized woman who bore us. Precisely because they are women, stepmothers must be gold-medal nurturers, regardless of what *they* want or are like as people.

Many stepmothers lament that stepfamily life is one big endurance test of meeting burdensome expectations. They sense the world at their backs, void of reasonable expectations,patience and interest in cutting stepmothers any breaks.

The litany of reproach they hear?

"So you're a stepmom . . . well then . . . *obviously* you like kids. And of *course* you are interested in being a homemaker. How soon before you finally set things right for your family? We expect *you*—no one else—to wipeout all the grief, disappointment, and hurt of divorce or death, to pull everyone together in a neat, tight bundleof familial harmony."

Meanwhile, though we expect much, we just don't believe that the stepmother can ever deliver. "How?" we scoff, especially in cases where a stepmom has not had children before. "Just look at her—what does she know about parenting?""

If a setting ever existed for someone to drive herself crazy (and to be driven nuts) trying to be Supermom, the cautionary accounts of stepmothers suggest stepfamily life is it. There are cases where stepmothers come into conflict with stepdaughters who have had most of dad's attention before he met his new mate. Yet, if the stepmoms try to compensate by being "a good mother," they run the risk of sparking fierce loyalty conflicts in their stepkids. Researcher Glenn Clingempeel studied stepkids age 9-12 and found that relations between daughters and stepmoms were the worst when new marriages were the best.

Indeed, stepmothering is tough going, even for those who succeed. "The kids didn't take well to someone new coming in and disciplining them," Bonnie recalls about her days before she got her poem of gratitude from her step-son. They resented it. Meanwhile, she was frustrated with her husband over the way their new household was run.

"We butted heads right away," Bonnie remembers. "I was used to not having to answer to anyone."

The real killer, though, is there is often no payoff for stepmothers who try to be all things to all people—no poems, no nothing. You can jump through ten, twenty, fifty hoops. Usually, the result is the same—"jump some more, ma'am."

So you do a reasonable job being in mom's shadow. "Big deal!" society says grudgingly. "You were supposed to do that anyway. All women are expected to able to care for a family."

And when things go wrong, you might have an alibi if you were a stepfather. Men are not regarded as naturally gifted at parenting. Because they live under lower expectations, they are often excused.

But a woman? The finger of blame points at your throat.

"People always assume you split up the first marriage," according to Carolyn, a stepmom who married a man who had two children. "They thought I had taken my stepkids from their mother. I actually had people say to me: 'How awful for the children not to be with their own mother.'" In response, Carolyn steeled herself and tried harder. She attempted to be absolutely wonderful and halfway succeeded, despite the challenges of early stepfamily life that even defeat perfectionists easily.

Still, it didn't quite work out. Carolyn just found herself in a tortuous Catch-22.

"The children expect you to be a mother," she says, "but when you act like one, they can't accept it. If I was being the best mother I could be, that turned out to be a problem.

"My stepkids wanted their own mother to be perfect—not me. If they liked what I was doing, they would catch themselves before they went too far because it made them feel disloyal to their own mom. My good effort was nothing but a source of confusion."

However, for many women, the pressures of stepmothering lie within as well as without. Stepmoms, especially women married for the first time, may have very unrealistic, romantic ideas about stepfamilies. They may believe mistakenly they are going to have their husbands to themselves, or they are going to feel love for their stepchildren—and vice versa.

It can be devastating when reality shows them otherwise. Some women begin to think something is innately wrong, and search desperately and vainly for ways to "fix" things, even though the confusion and unrest at home is normal.

"If I had already been used to the calamity and insanity of it all, it would have helped," reported one stepmother who, at age 35 and with no parenting experience, married a man who had two very young children. She added: "If I had my own children, it would have appeared more equal. But as it was, it seemed so one-sided."

Worse, stepmoms who have difficulties begin to think *they* are the source of trouble and fall headfirst into a downward spiral of destructive self-doubt and self-criticism.

"Where did *I* go wrong?" cries the stepmom, hardly the lament of Cinderella's cruel stepmother.

You can help yourself if you try not to live up to any one else's expectations or put excessive and unrealistic demands on yourself. If you fail to measure up, you may be wracked by self-doubt, a condition unhelpful to effective stepparenting.

Instead, stay focused on developing your own unique relationship with your stepchildren and the valuable part you can play in their lives.

The Supermom Syndrome—A Closer Look

Lynne had been married twice before, but she had never had children of her own. So it was quite a change when, seven years ago, she married a man with an eight-year-old daughter. Lynne threw herself into her stepmothering, with the blessing of her husband who gave her carte blanche to run the household. A truckdriver, he was absent regularly for long periods.

Burning with a Supermom's sense of mission, Lynne tried to take control of her new household.

"I like structure," she says. "I set up rules."There was one problem, though—weak support and contradictory parenting from her husband and his ex, the "Kryptonite" that saps the strength of many a Supermom in the world of stepfamilies.

"It took me a year before I realized I wasn't getting anywhere," Lynne remembers. "My stepdaughter would test me constantly and get away with it. Worse, my husband wouldn't do anything about it. He just didn't want to be a 'bad guy' in his daughter's eyes. I would tell him he didn't have to say I was right. All he had to do was say something like 'uh-huh' to things I said to my stepdaughter. But he wouldn't even do that. It got to be ridiculous. Whenever he failed to support me, he would say 'You said everything that needs to be said.' He just refused to speak up and take charge."

Lynne says discustedly of her partner's ex-wife, "She imposed no rules on my stepdaughter in her household." "She wasn't a parent. She was quick to side with her dauhgter in everything."

After five trying years of stepmotherhood, Lynne's stepdaughter—by then a teenager—uttered the words few people want to hear from a child they parent.

"She said she didn't like me and she wanted to move in with her mother," Lynne recalls. Tensions got so high "I threatened my husband with separation."

Today, Lynne still feels like the "wicked stepmother," though she has been able to undo one shoulderstrap on her Supermom cape. Her lobbying for support finally worked, she says; her husband has become a more active parent.

"He handles my stepdaughter now," Lynne says. "He sits down and talks to her, and makes it clear there are consequences for certain behaviors. He has let her know she isn't the equal of adults in the house."

Reflecting on her experience, Lynne believes this is the way things should have been from the start. She admits making the mistake of coming on too strong. As an outsider, it was wrong to charge forward, trying to bring order, she says; instead, she should have held off. Possibly she had moments as unforgiving judge and jury on the parenting around her. Reduced to being on standby by their outsider status, some stepparents act like hyper-critical observers, picking apart everything in sight. Typically, disharmony results.

But it is also true that Lynne had no choice but to think she could do things better. Her husband's negligence helped force her to try to take on the role of Supermom.

"If I had to do it over again, I would not get so directly involved," Lynne says now.

Details may differ, but interviews with other stepmothers suggest that what happened to Lynne is, at root, an all-too-familiar story.

"My kids need a mother—you're it. Take over. Make things right. Do something." This is what partners often say directly or indirectly to stepmothers.

"As a general rule, stepmothers shouldn't get too involved right away," cautions Norma Campbell, a therapist and stepmother. "Sometimes, fathers promote this. They want the stepmother to make up for the failings or the absence of the children's actual mother, or they want the reconstituted family to be happy.

"Directly or indirectly, the stepmother is put in the position of having to give a lot. She must have a good relationship with her stepkids and help them through all the tension and conflict that is characteristic of early stepfamilies. That's a difficult role for anyone to be in, especially since the stepchild has parents already."

Campbell could have been thinking of Della, a stepmom for nearly a decade. Della thinks she has a better relationship with her stepdaughter than does her husband, a busy insurance broker who typically gets home late only to be back out on the job early the next morning.

"He does try to call from around the country, but if I asked him to do more, it would be asking a lot," Della says. "It's a personal frustration of mine. I understand his situation, but that doesn't make things any easier here at home."

Pushed by spouses, women pressure themselves with their own high expectations. Campbell adds, "Working hasn't changed women's proclivity to do this. It is an emotional thing."

Marion, a stepmother of two older children, concurs. "Society assumes we have to take over, and our husbands let us," she says. "Even in this age of more assertive women, biological fathers do not take on the parenting chores in a remarriage.

Somehow, we women believe it is our responsibility. Ours is a false belief."

Marion hit turbulence when she began to run her household. Her teenage stepson resented her ways and rebelled. He had lived with his father before she married him; the kid was used to a more relaxed parenting style.

Marion teaches stepparenting classes and says many students show up worn-out, frustrated Supermoms, each with her cape snagged on the same trap. The solution to this situation lies in resisting external and internal pressures to be the perfect everything to everyone. Bonnie received her stepson's poem partly because she never tried to do it all. Also, others in her stepfamily took on some responsibilities. With five kids, ages three to fourteen, Bonnie and her husband carefully worked out a plan for all the children to do their own assigned chores. Everything does not automatically fall on mom's shoulders this way, and kids get to do their part.

"They probably have more responsibility than if they were in a biological family," Bonnie says. "They help with the house and do yardwork. The oldest ones help take care of the younger ones."

You will also avoid the burden of being Supermom if you accept your stepchildren, realizing that they have had lives which had nothing to do with you. Their pre-established connections and previous experiences are going to influence their behavior.

"It's terribly important to recognize that stepfamily relationships come from loss," observes Sally, a stepmother to boys ages seven and ten. "Everyone is hurting and scared some. You must deal with that and be honest about it, from the adults down to toddlers."

Sally consciously pulled herself back from the brink of taking on too much responsibility for her stepkids.

"I had to think—I'm not their mother," she says about what it was like to care at first for her husband's two young children who visited every other week. "They had a mother whom I couldn't compete with or replace."

Sally encouraged everyone in her stepfamily to discuss their feelings. She says the tactic countered her husband's tendency to "gloss over everything" and also addressed some very personal issues. Her own twelve-year-old daughter had a stepfather before, hadn't liked him, and was unaccepting when Sally first started going out with her current spouse.

"She thought I shouldn't date until my younger child had grown." But it helped to talk things out. Relations remain difficult between Sally's daughter and her stepfather, but there are small signs of improvement.

"Once she wouldn't even visit," Sally says, "but she's started to come around. She sees things aren't terrible. I'm happy."

As a stepmother, you simply can't do it all. Your partner is going to have to be supportive and reasonable. You must realize that your stepchildren are connected to a past that has nothing to do with you, and everything to do with them and their behavior. So don't expect your stepkids to be perfect, imposing impossible standards on them. And encourage open and honest communication with your husband and among family members. Talking things out will help everyone be more accepting and stay focused on your future together.

FRIENDSHIP SHOULD BE THE GOAL

A slice of gallows humor is what Catherine remembers best about the first stages of stepmotherhood.

"I used to say I had a love-hate relationship with my stepdaughter," she says. "I loved—she hated."

Life was no joke, however. Everything "went to hell" for two years as Catherine and her stepdaughter squared off whenever the girl would visit. Much of the animosity was a clash over loyalties, fed by the girl's mother. It contrasted sharply with Catherine and her husband's dating days.

"In the beginning we were good friends," Catherine says of her pre-marriage relations with her stepdaughter. "But there was a definite point after my husband and I married when she changed. She would say she hated me and our house. It didn't help that my husband's ex really sunk her teeth into making trouble, too."

Catherine says she felt rejected and without any control over the situation. She compares the time to feeling like "an animal trapped in a corner."

Tensions eased after the family sought therapy and the ex got distracted with a new man in her life. The counseling served to relieve the pressure and guilt Catherine had put on herself because she did not feel very loving toward her stepdaughter.

"I realized I wasn't required to feel any way," she says, thinking of the agony she put herself through because she felt so inadequate.

Despite all the turmoil she endured, Catherine is among the lucky few. Many stepmothers never have the same awakening. The result is devastating, particularly for people who have never been parents and make the mistake of putting their pent up need to be loved as mothers on the thin shoulders of stepchildren. Their problems only compound when their yearnings for a love relationship with their stepkids are fueled by spouses with a demanding "love me—love my children" attitude.

Right now, you may be standing with your toes over the edge of the same pitfall. You sense obvious need. You see stepkids who have had a rough time; they may have endured years of neglect and unhappiness, and seem like prime candidates for a mother's warm, tender love.

In a situation like that it is best to be cognizant of an unavoidable fact: ultimately, you probably will never love your stepchildren as you would your own kids—nor will they love you as a natural mother.

Don't let this possibility drive you to feel guilty, however, or beat yourself up, as it did Catherine. The absence of love between stepmother and stepchildren is normal. All the motherly love you may feel can never wipe out the separate histories, divided loyalties and other unique features of stepfamily life that prevent automatic love relationships between stepparents and stepkids.

Unless you are in a unique situation—for example, your

children are very young and do not have a mother—chances are very good that you won't have the closeness of traditional mother-child relationships.

This prospect is not as bleak as it may sound, however. Stepmothers who have experienced Catherine's awakening have felt unburdened.

"One stepmother told me it was the most liberating information she had ever gotten," therapist Miriam Galper Cohen told the *Ladies' Home Journal* in an article titled, "Step-by-Step Parenthood."

Keep in mind, too, that some of the flak you encounter from your stepkids could have nothing to do with the question of love. Stepmothers without any parenting experience may have a difficult time understanding this. They have never been exposed to the tantrums and quirky behavior of kids growing up. Or it may be that your stepchildren are used to being on their own and dislike the idea of another adult looking after them.

"My stepdaughter was at a real combustible age," Catherine notes. "Some of what happened was just a reflection of her adolescence. However, I had never been through that with a kid before. If I had, I might have looked at her, said 'Oh well,' and walked away. Instead, a lot of the time I blew things up into a stepfamily crisis."

"I thought the problem was that I wasn't accepting enough because I had never had any children," adds another stepmother who eventually learned to lose her feelings of inadequacy.

It helps to have a realistic talk with your stepkids which throws a light on the common ground between you, despite the absence of love.

For example, you might say, "I respect the fact that you don't want another parent in your life right now, but I just want you to know that I'm willing to take an interest in your life if you wish. You can consider me a good friend."

To help clarify what you have mind, call to mind the behavior of a good adult family friend, an aunt, a godmother who is liked by your stepchild. Also, be honest about love.

"Love? Well, we may not love each other, but there is someone around here whom we both can agree deserves our love: your father. For the time being, can't we resolve whatever differences we have for the sake of his happiness?"

Whatever you do, keep those communication lines open.

Also, you and your stepchildren can take steps towards a friendship through shared activities. That is what was done by Linda, who had never cared for a child when she became a nine-year-old boy's stepmother. The child lived with her and her husband half of the time. Linda started simply, stuffing Christmas stockings with her stepson. Other ideas include playing parlor games together(on the same team); attending your stepchildrens' school activities; helping them with homework assignments here and there; watching a movie together; and making their favorite dish occasionally.

But you cannot expect a short path to a better relationship. Patience and tolerance with imperfection in your stepkids and yourself will be necessary. If you are too rigid, you risk venting frustration on your stepchildren, and the damage from that can be swift and great.

"Everything you do and say can be wiped out with one bad event," according to Della, the stepmom with the insurance broker spouse. She preaches setting realistic goals and keeping your eyes on them, no matter what. "You have to decide what works for you and stick with it."

The most important thing to remember about step-motherhood and love is to never feel that you must love your stepkids and be loved by them in return. That will put undue pressure on your relationship. By taking a more measured and relaxed approach, it may be possible for a good friendship to develop—no small achievement in any type of adult-child relationship

Your stepchildren may not love you, nor you them, but you must not conclude that it is okay for you to wash your hands completely of all parenting. "I didn't have to be mom, but I still had to be an adult," notes Linda, a stepmother in California.

It would be foolish of you to demand respect because you are the "mother." Work on being a good friend first. As the *step*mother, you must earn your stepchildren's trust with your actions. You have to show that your interest in them is genuine. But you should be treated politely and with consideration, too. If your stepchildren fail in this regard, your spouse should take the lead in disciplining them, making it clear that you deserve better.

Forget the love stuff, though. Instead, be *loving*—warm, kind, patient and understanding.

"You enter stepmotherhood wanting to be a parent, and you want to be thought of as a parent—but that rarely happens," Della warns. "At first, the children will resent you. The best possible situation is to be an adult friend."

VISITING STEPCHILDREN— YOU NEED MORE THAN A WELCOME MAT

Recent shifts in legal approaches are creating more opportunities for men to gain custody of their children. Nevertheless, it is still very common for stepmoms to be married to someone whose kids live with their mother and who are occasional visitors at dad's for limited periods of time. If you are in this situation, there is plenty to consider and plan for.

For instance, if the new stepmother and her partner are settling in nicely. The stepmom may still cling to romantic dreams about her new life—notions with no trace of the very unromantic work involved in having children around under any circumstances. Her reverie ends, however, when the stepchildren arrive. The kids enter resentful, uncommunicative and uncomfortable in the new setting. Also, certain aspects of their appearances may tug at the stepmom's maternal heartstrings. Perhaps the kids are badly dressed or unclean or show other evidence of neglect or mistreatment.

From guilt, genuine concern, insecurity or a mix of all three, the stepmother feels obligated to change everything quickly. She is nervous about whether her home is "right" for her stepchildren, forgetting that the quality of the personal interaction during their time with her will be more important than any setting. Mistakenly, the visit seems to her like an opportunity to be not Mom or even Supermom, but Super-Supermom!

So the stepmother throws herself into pulling off the perfect visit, kidding herself that she can single-handedly, in a brief period of time, wipe away a real and painful past. Though she may barrage her stepchildren with attention, they stand as unresponsive as statues.

"Who is this phony?" the besieged stepchildren wonder. "She doesn't know us or what we like. She's just someone who has gotten between us and our father,.and between our father and mother, and now she's trying to make up for that with this big show of attention. The biggest joke is that she's never had kids of her own,so what does she know?

As the visit unfolds, the stepchildren act like full-blown takers—not givers. They accept spoiling from the step-mother, but show no appreciation. Worse, they command Dad's attention an time. It becomes starkly, even painfully, clear that the stepmom is out of touch with an important part of her partner's life.

There is an entire side to him that did not include her, still does not, and may never; tending to his children dis-tracts him from her and her needs. Discouragingly, as the visits go on, it appears that the husband will be distracted indefinitely.

Boiled down, the sudden, exclusive togetherness between him and his visiting children is a threat at worst, annoying at best. The father spoils his kids, too, and the step-mother, though she is blind to her own drive for perfection, criticizes this as poor parenting.

"How can he give those little twits so much attention and ignore me?" she seethes.

If the stepmom has her own kids living with her, there may be other worries. Her children could be unwelcoming and resent any attention paid the visiting stepchildren. They may balk at being pressured to share with and like kids they neither know nor have any feelings for. Antagonisms could develop between the two sets of children which could draw in the parents and start to divide them, too.

The whole visit becomes a trial and detours the development of the stepfamily. It turns off the children involved, serves as a source of friction between the adults and leaves the stepmother feeling acutely rejected, alone and helpless.

Obviously, none of this sounds very encouraging. Yet, the visits of stepchildren can be made tolerable and even enjoyable.

Much of the responsibility of planning should belong to your partner as parent of the children in question. As a rule, unless stepchildren are teens, parents should do the planning so children are not caught in the middle. But stepparents do need to be involved to some extent. You and your partner should communicate closely about visits and prepare for them together.

Here are some suggestions for making your role most effective. To some extent, they hinge on the ages of the kids; however, each one has some universal application:

◆　◆　◆

Be prepared for your stepchildren's frame of mind, and understand the reason for it. Remember where they came from prior to walking through your door. They could be influenced or even coached by your partner's ex to have a negative image of you or to give you a hard time.

They may wear the face of rejection as a defense mechanism because they are unsure of their new environment and you. They could be afraid or be restrained by guilt from smiling and appearing to enjoy their visit because that would seem disloyal to their mother.

Indeed, your visiting stepchildren's insecurities over being uprooted and thrust into a new home are going to be most acute when they first arrive—and when they depart Experienced stepparents say it is wise to allow step-kids to "decompress" during post-arrival and pre-departure hours. Leave well enough alone while they sort out their feelings and try to figure out for themselves where they belong. Hold off and ease the children into the atmosphere and routine of your home.

Try stopping at a neutral site like a restaurant when you pick up the children to help them gather themselves and to slow and ease the transition to the new household.

You should also allow time for them to get ready to return to their place of residence. Some youngsters withdraw when they realize that they have yet another transition to make.

"My stepson was feeling real good, like he was part of the family. He had an ideal situation," Angela says about her stepchild's uneasiness at the conclusion of his summer-long visit in her home. "So it was hard for him to leave. Things at his mom's were definitely different."

At such times, you would be ill-advised to get critical, upset or interfering. Your stepchildren's behavior will be normal, therefore, let it be. Generally, the same advice applies if your stepchildren are visitors in the other household. Ease off as the time comes for them to leave for Dad's or Mom's. They could be pretty anxious.

Do not attempt to use your stepchildren to send advice or critical messages back to the absent parent. That would be unfair to your stepchildren and could spark conflict between households.

◆　◆　◆

Manage the visit to a reasonable goal. You don't want your stepchildren to be bowled over with attention or spoiled. The "perfect weekend trap" springs when step-families give in to feelings of insecurity and ease discipline to guarantee a good time for visiting stepchildren so they will want to return. That is not a very realistic or good method of parenting. It may also hurt the parenting of the ex, who could feel pressured to spoil in turn. In addition, there are practical considerations to weigh. It can very expensive to entertain children these days. You don't want your stepchildren in the habit of expecting your family to spend a lot of money on them every time they visit.

During visits, you want interaction that is in balance. Act as though your stepchildren are people who live with you, though under more limited circumstances. Make them feel as though they are family, with all the privileges and responsibilities of all other family members. The welcome at your house should reflect that—no more, no less.

Visiting kids who are allowed to play while stepsiblings do chores stand a good chance of being resented. It may be fitting, however, to exempt your stepchildren from chores if their visits are infrequent. Much will depend on how often they are at your home. If they are with you regularly, it would be wiser to make your stepchildren realize that they will not be spoiled or treated differently than anyone else. The experience can teach them maturity.

However, no one should interpret this call for realism and moderation as an excuse to be aloof. You don't want your visiting stepkids to feel ignored and isolated. Sometimes, parents think it is sufficient just to be in the same residence with their visiting children. They put them in front of the TV for the entire visit, and leave it at that. No one interacts. This is the opposite extreme of the "perfect weekend trap" and it also will not suffice. Balance is everything.

✦   ✦   ✦

Know something about your stepchildren ahead of time. What are their interests? What kind of food do they like? Based on the information you get, plan activities that show you care.

Through phone calls, letters or contact with the other parent, if possible, make sure your stepchildren know something in advance about your home, the people in it and the developments there. For example, inform them in advance that you and their father are planning to have their favorite dish one night; you could ease some of their apprehension that way, and possibly make them view their visit with greater anticipation. Report on what their room looks like, so they are somewhat oriented before they arrive. If a major distraction is underway—say you're remodeling your home—warn them that people's attention may have to be a bit diverted during their visit. This extra effort should reduce the chances of your stepkids' feeling slighted once they arrive.

Your partner may want to encourage his children to bring something for the stepsiblings as a sign of friendship. Gradually, too, as everyone becomes more comfortable with the visits, perhaps the stepchildren could be allowed to bring their own friends with them as another way of making them feel at home.

Make sure your own kids are prepared for the visit. Let them know what is going on, but don't put pressure them to act any certain way. Instead, encourage them to be as accepting and cooperative as possible.

One way to accomplish this would be to have them make or buy a welcoming gift to present to their new stepsiblings: a baseball, a bike accessory, a book, a CD or video. Have your children introduce them to friends in the neighborhood or at school. They may also want to call or write just to say hello. In any case, reassure them that the visit doesn't mean that they have lost their special status with you in any way.

✦　　✦　　✦

Give your visiting stepchildren something to call their own—a room, a drawer, a toy, a game, sporting goods or clothing. Make sure there is a spot in the bathroom with toiletries for them, so they can come without having too much to pack. Have these things available and ready always. This will also help your stepchildren feel more accepted in their new environment, and demonstrate your seriousness in regarding them as family.

Other tips could include displaying photos of non-resident stepchildren in your home or, when the time is right, have a family photo taken which includes them and display it prominently and proudly. Have extra prints made up and make it a point to tell your stepchildren that you are going to be giving them to their stepgrandparents and other extended family members.

Also, you may want to invite family, friends and neighbors over to visit and be introduced. Do this to the appropriate degree, however. You do not want your stepchildren to feel you have no interest in others knowing about their visit, but neither do you want to put them on display and make them feel uncomfortable.

✦　✦　✦

Let your stepchildren have an equal say in planning their visits. Contact them directly by telephone calls or by writing to them. Inform them ahead of time about changes in plans or family discussions about future activities.

Do not take your stepchildren for granted by burdening them with schedules and details for weekends and vacations, especially when other children have had a say in planning. That could make them feel coerced and unequal.

✦　✦　✦

Expect and accept that your spouse's attention will be diverted when your stepchildren arrive. Don't mope; take action. It will help if you have interests of your own to pursue while your spouse and his child spend time together.

Sometimes when stepchildren bring friends along, they take up time that would otherwise be spent with Dad. This will allow your partner to be with you and curb your feelings of being left out.

You can also try spending time with your stepchildren, gradually laying down the basis of a relationship with them. It may be that your spouse is the one who feels more uncomfortable around his kids. Perhaps the past contains a lot of hurt. In that case, you have to be more involved than you expected.

Can you match any of your skills and interests with your stepchildren's? Do you share their interest in games, movies or sports? Do you have any special skills they might be interested in learning? Cooking? Fishing? Carpentry? Pick one and pursue it.

Whatever you do, make it clear that your stepchildren are welcome in your home. Do not expect a tremendous response. Your time together may seem inconsequential, but you may have more of an impact than you realize. Sometimes kids are unexpressive, even though they appreciate what is being done for them.

♦ ♦ ♦

Stay in close touch with your spouse and be honest about your feelings. Solicit his advice for the best methods of approaching your stepchildren. Be honest if you feel the onus for preparing and planning the visits is being put on you, yet you are also being cut out of things once your stepchildren arrive. Work together to make sure visits go smoothly and tensions are minimized.

If your stepchildren will be visiting, you need to be prepared for their frame of mind, and be understanding of it. They could arrive feeling like outsiders. They may be anxious or unsettled, so give them a chance to ease into the life of your new household. Do not besiege them with attention, but set reasonable goals for their visit and give them responsibilities if circumstances allow. Prepare your kids for their stepsiblings' visit, and give your stepchildren a say in planning their visits and some idea what will happen. Accept that your partner may be distracted from you while his stepkids are around, too. Work closely with him— cooperation is the key to making the visits successful.

Part Four...
Stepchildren

Who is this person to divert my mother (or father) from me?

Why must I give up my friends, my neighborhood and my school in order to move in with a bunch of people I don't even know or like?

This stepfamily business is not my idea . . .

Welcome to the mindset of stepchildren.

For openers, you and your stepkids will probably be at cross-purposes. Do not panic or become discouraged, though, as conflict is a normal and understandable occurrence in a stepfamily situation.

Presumably, you and your partner love each other. As a couple, you are going about the exciting business of planning a new life together. Personally, you feel liberated. The loneliness you felt when you were single has departed. Life seems brighter, easier and more controllable. Your confidence and self-esteem are up, courtesy of new-found love. You feel more open, giving and secure. Your partner gives you moral and practical support.

In addition, your stepfamily represents a precious second chance—an opportunity for you and your spouse to close the book on disappointment and heartache. Finally, you think, you have the family that has eluded you.

So what could be wrong with such a picture? "Everything," your stepchildren might say. In a nutshell, your happiness could be their grief. Many children think their world is falling apart when their stepfamily forms. They may hold stepparents responsible for the breakup of their parents' marriage or they may regard them as intruders.

Unlike you with your plans for the future, stepchildren usually do not like to look ahead—they look back, often to a past they idealize. They may stay loyal to that past. This is a chief reason why you must not commit the stepparenting sins of openly belittling your stepchildrens' outside parent, or putting down components of their past like their old neighborhood or school.

Stepchildren often have difficulty getting as starry-eyed as adults about such concepts as unity and togetherness. Frequently, they enter stepfamilies burned by disappointment and heartache. Though young, they have had their fill of divorce, death or breakups. For whatever reason, the adults in their lives have failed to deliver on their promises.

Many stepchildren have been confused enough by shuttling back and forth between custodial and non-custodial households during their pre-stepfamily days. However, their confusion may acquire a new dimension when their stepfamily forms and sets up living quarters in a new place. Your stepchildren may move in with the outlook and attitude of unsettled, powerless outsiders in a home full of strangers.

Caught up in these emotions, stepchildren often adopt goals that conflict with adults'.Some set out to make sure the stepfamily fails. They see that as the solution to reuniting mom and dad, restoring their importance to their custodial parent and returning to the pre-stepfamily days they idealize. However, none of this excuses bad behavior or disrespect on the part of stepchildren. Every stepparent deserves fair and polite treatment.

When you consider the adjustments that stepchildren have to make, negative stereotypes of them seem very shallow, if not downright cruel. Remember, they are children. By taking time to look more closely at why your stepkids act the way they do, you will promote a family environment that is more understanding.

Naturally, not all situations will be alike. The degree of stepparent-stepchild conflict in your new home will vary. In every case, you must work hard in order to practice good stepparenting. You can never sit back and expect everything to fall into place on its own.

VERY YOUNG STEPCHILDREN—GIVE PEACE A CHANCE

To help the development of very young stepchildren, strive for a household free of conflict, guilt and confusion. Do not pretend to be a traditional family. Since your stepchildren don't have the obvious loyalties of older kids, you may think you can act as though your stepfamily has been one, big happy family all along. This may cause stepchildren to believe that you are somehow ashamed of being in a stepfamily. It may also lead to confusion, anger and resentment toward the stepparent as they grow and gradually understand the truth.

Instead, be honest. Using a balanced approach, help your stepkids to understand the need for custodial and non-custodial households. Do not require them to call you "mom" or "dad." That could be interpreted as being highly inappropriate by the outside parent. Try a substitute such as using "mom" or "dad" as a prefix to your first name. It shows that you are not interested in taking over someone else's children, and that you are serious about raising them as openly as possible.

Encourage relations between your stepchildren and their absent parent. Be wary of immediately assuming full parenting duties. Hopefully, your stepchildren have a caring mother or father. By intervening too much or too soon, you may cause conflict between yourself and that parent. The right kind of contact with the absent parent will protect and nurture your stepchildrens' self-esteem and identity.

You should develop your own relationship with each stepchild. Do not discourage contact between your stepchildren and their outside parent.

Unfortunately, some stepparents who cannot manage to look beyond their own needs sometimes put stepkids in the difficult position of having to choose between households. For example, they may ask the children, "Wouldn't you rather be with us this Christmas?" or, "You don't want to leave us and go to your dad's, do you?"

As you can imagine, saying such things to a young child can force them to make painful decisions. When choices must be made, listen fairly to your stepchildren. Discuss matters privately with your partner, then decide jointly on a plan that reflects your stepchildrens' interests. As much as possible, households should work as a team on handling visits.

Take appropriate interest in your stepchildren. Devote time to them. Actively follow and monitor their interests, activities, schooling and health. Also, allow them to have input in stepfamily decisions. For example, do not rush into adopting your stepchild. Do not assume you can substitute your surname for theirs. Do not preclude giving them a voice about visits. Try to determine what your stepchildren want and how they feel—then act accordingly. Parent in their best interests, not yours.

Stepfathers should not leave daily childcare duties to their partners. If you feel inadequate raising young children, you can read self-help books for tips or sign up for parenting classes. Consider lending a hand as an opportunity to bond with your stepchildren and set a good example for them.

Don't forget your older stepchildren. Your youngest stepchildren may appear to need more attention. They may be more responsive to you and therefore it may seem more rewarding to parent them. They may throw their arms around you, laugh at your teasing and generally be less guarded. The net result is that they could easily appear more likeable.

Do not let this appearance distract you, however. Your older stepchildren will need you, too, despite appearing comparatively unreceptive to your overtures. The methods may differ, but the fact remains that you have some stepparenting to do with each child.

ADULT STEPCHILDREN: ANOTHER CHALLENGE

Adult stepchildren may be better prepared than their younger siblings are for the ambiguities of stepfamily life. Usually, they are more secure than younger people, and their emotional constitutions are stronger. They may be independent from their parents and be glad mom or dad has a new partner, seeing it as important companionship for a lonely parent. It could ease their worry about mom or dad living alone.

Yet, pitfalls can await. If you stepparent adults, you are not necessarily "home free." Your partner's children could be overprotective, for example. They may suspect you married mom or dad for some ulterior motive—money, perhaps, or maybe for comfortable but loveless companionship. Their suspicions could make you feel as though you must continuously prove your intentions. Meanwhile, the children could make themselves feel insecure; for instance, they could worry needlessly that you are a threat to their inheritance.

If you marry a widow or widower, your problems could even be more intense. In word and deed, your stepchildren could tell you that they think you will never measure up to the standards set by their dear, departed mom or dad. Their attitude could cause you much frustration. You may feel powerless and unappreciated as you are forced to compete with the idealized ghost of the deceased parent.

And there are other potential troublespots. For instance, remarrying may change a lifestyle in which your stepchildren were secure. No longer do they feel completely comfortable just dropping in on their parent. The interests or hobbies they might have shared and pursued together now have to be put on hold. They could resent you for causing change and diverting their parent's attention away from them.

You can preclude, prepare for and weather such storms successfully by taking approaches such as the following:

Be an active and aware stepparent. If your stepchildren live elsewhere than in your home, they may seem invisible. It is even more important, in this case, that you acknowledge that they *are* part of your partner's life, and always will be. You cannot deny this.

For true family harmony, you and your stepchildren will at least have to have cordial relations. You can contribute by taking a reasonable interest in their lives, communicating with them regularly and letting them know you welcome them in your new life and home.

With many years together, adult stepchildren's ties to their parents can be very strong. If that is so in your case, there will probably be plenty of times when you feel like an outsider. You may have to reconcile yourself to hearing stories about not only your spouse, but also the absent parent.

Be patient and understanding, though. If you feel insecure or jealous and are tempted to limit your partner's availability to your stepkids, do not. Instead, use your circumstances as a chance to shine. Show that you are secure enough to listen to the talk about the past, have no interest in obstructing good times and are willing to share your spouse's attention. Ideally, your stepchildren will appreciate your generous approach and be more inclined to accept you.

Be mindful that your stepchildren are adults, with set loyalties to the past and independent lives to lead. Avoid putting your stepchildren under the weight of absurd expectations, such as calling you "mom" or "dad,", or obeying you because you think of yourself as their father or mother. You will need to be much more open and flexible. To keep from giving the impression of taking over, and to make known your good intentions, involve your stepchildren as much as possible in decisions which touch on the past.

For instance, as noted previously , let them know in advance if you have plans for redecorating their childhood home. Before you sell or give away items of sentimental value, discuss your intentions with your stepkids, and give them a chance to claim them.

As a courtesy, too, you and your spouse may want to get your stepchildrens' opinions about changes you contemplate making in your wills or other planning documents. Inform them of your final decisions once they are made, so that everyone is clear on where things stand and are not surprised later on. Your spouse should take the lead in settling strong disagreements in order to protect you from possible recriminations.

Be patient with your stepchildren's grief over a deceased parent. Bereavement has no defined limits. People grieve in different ways and for different periods of time. Thus, saying something like, "Isn't it about time you moved on?" to your stepchildren is both callous and wrong. People do not move away from grief on predetermined schedules.

A better approach would be to say, "I respect your parent's memory. I know your dad (or mom) meant a lot to you, and I share your sorrow. I can't replace your parent, but I would like to be friends, if you'll give me the chance."

On the flip side, you need not subject yourself to unreasonable comparisons with the life led by the deceased, constantly living with the onus of having to prove yourself. If you do begin to feel inferior, talk your feelings out with your spouse in confidence *before* you explode with frustration. You must be accepted for who you are.

Comparisons with and reminders of a deceased parent are unavoidable to some degree. Stay calm when this happens, and try not to take the behavior too personally. More important is that your spouse accept you, and that you have a solid partnership. That support should give you the confidence you need to deal with your stepchildren until they begin to appreciate you for yourself.

Be aware that live-at-home adult stepchildren may present you with a very big challenge, especially in the area of control. Because of their long family standing and their age, your live-at-home adult stepchildren may consider themselves your equal, if not your superior, in how things are run around the house. More set in their ways than younger stepkids and more tied to home, they may feel even more threatened and defensive about your "invading" their space.

You, on the other hand, may have your own frustrations. As a daily witness to the bond between your partner and your adult stepchildren, you may feel quite powerless. With nothing to compare to their extended history together, your feelings of being an outsider may be very sharp indeed.

In addition, because your stepchildren are adults, you and your partner may find it harder to control their behavior. You could have trouble being heard or getting privacy with your spouse.

What is the solution? Be sure you and your mate are in agreement that the two of you are the foundation of your new stepfamily. Once that is clear, encourage your partner to convey your position to your stepchildren, and to confirm it with example. He or she should be diplomatic but firm.

A suggested approach would be to say, "Your stepdad (or stepmom) is the new dad(or mom) in this house. I ask that you respect this situation. This does not mean that you are unwanted, must leave or don't have any more say in how things run around here. You should have some input and we do want you to stay. But I am asking you to accept this change and to behave accordingly. You mean a great deal to me—and to your new stepparent."

Chances are this shift in power will be more acceptable if news of it reaches your stepkids before you ever live with them. That will allow for discussion and reduce the chance of them seeing any change as too sudden or a betrayal.

Assert yourself in your new household gradually. If need be, focus on a couple of modest rules for enforcement, rather than pushing for wholesale change that would completely wipe out the way things have always been. Concentrate, too, on making arrangements for you and your spouse to achieve what is so crucial to couples in step-families—time alone.

Be diligent about going out periodically, if necessary, to get your privacy. At home, check calendars with your stepchildren to find out when the house is free and there is a block of time to have friends over without inconveniencing anyone or creating friction. Seek your stepchildren's opinions on household matters in sincere but non-binding ways, such as, "We are gathering ideas about painting the rec room. What are your thoughts?" (Imply that their answer will be one of several that will be considered.) Another approach would be to say, "Your Dad (Mom) and I have decided to paint the rec room. Would you like to help us pick out a color?" (You are in control of the decision, but your stepchildren have a voice.) Once your stepkids sense that you are well-intended and have good judgement, they may drop their defenses and relinquish control.

If they decide on their own to move out, make it clear that the decision is theirs and that they are welcome to come back if they wish. When their leaving seems like a potential solution to family discord, have your partner talk to your stepchildren first, giving them time to shape up.

Should the worst case scenario develop—if nothing changes and they must be asked to move out—you and your mate should approach the matter as positively as possible. Treat the separation a something for everyone's good—for the sake of family togetherness, rather than as punishment directed at anyone.

Tell your stepchildren that there are no hard feelings, that you will be happy to assist with the move any way you can and that they will always be welcome to visit.

Realize that having adult stepchildren can be very rewarding. Because of their age and maturity, it is possible that your stepchildren will be able to separate reason and emotion and accept you sooner than you think—sooner than younger stepchildren would. Perhaps they could see you as the person who finally gives mom the kind treatment she deserves, or dad the loving attention he needs—rather than as someone with selfish ulterior motives.

Hold on and try to be as hopeful as possible. You may not be too far removed from the start of a very meaningful adult friendship, courtesy of your stepchildren.

THE HOT SPOT: PRE-TEEN AND TEENAGE STEPCHILDREN

Stepkids ages nine to fifteen pose the biggest challenge for stepparents. It is the time when all children develop their identity and self-esteem. Thus, at this age, they are vulnerable and sensitive to dramatic changes in their family structure and living situations.

Stepparents of older children can face problems at two distinct levels, then. First, they must contend with what could be called pure stepfamily issues: inner conflicts your stepchildren suffer as they try to sort out how they feel about you, their insecurity over being supplanted by the formation of the stepfamily, and their distress from shuffling between households, to cite a few examples.

Meanwhile, you have a pre-teen or young teenager with whom you must deal. Many moms and dads will tell you *that*, in itself, can be your biggest difficulty. Serious developmental issues befall teenage stepchildren near or in the teen years because of their age, not because they are stepkids. They have their sexual awakenings, become more independent and experiment with behaviors which can seem strange, silly, even dangerous.

Parenting kids this age has never been easy. However, some recent developments—the upswing in violence among young people, a rise in teen suicide and substance abuse, and the threat of AIDS facing anyone who fails to treat sex responsibly—have made the job harder and much more worrisome.

Still, the root of conflict between stepparents and pre-teen and teenage stepchildren often lies at a basic level. Like every adult, you are what many kids in this age bracket think they need least: another embodiment of authority and rules. Furthermore, you probably have values and interests which, in the lingo of youth, can only be termed "uncool."

"Mom and Dad? Family gatherings? Togetherness and unity? Yeeeeeeeeeeeeeeeeeech!"

This could very well be your stepchildren's attitude toward family matters. You also stand a good chance of hearing them make declarations like these:

"I want to be free and independent. I want to be able to spend time with my friends. I should be able to come and go as I please. Why can't I say out late? My friends don't have rules. They say I'm crazy for listening to you."

Breaking loose from family is a normal part of teenage life. Stepchildren are no exception: they want to do their own thing; run free; be left alone. To a certain extent, they should be allowed some private time, a sort of escape valve for the pressures of growing up in modern society.

You could not pick a tougher age to parent. Stepkids in this age bracket are tailor-made to frustrate both stepparents who crack the whip and expect obedience, and those who harbor fantasies of experiencing instant mutual love with their stepkids.

Given such a tall order then, how do you proceed? How can you be most effective? Some recommendations that were mentioned in previous chapters have a particular urgency with this age group:

✦ *Keep expectations low, patience high.*

If you want to avoid great frustration, try not to expect too much from your stepkids—or your ability to influence them. Do not be put off by their failure to respond to you in the way *you* expect or want.

They are probably going to be far from sharing your dreams of a big, happy stepfamily. They may be wary about the adult world and unwilling to trust you. They may also differ greatly from you in temperament, interests, values and habits.

Avoid thinking of your stepkids as "disappointing" to you. Remember: you did not raise them; they are not yours. Your situation is such that there is no real basis for your stepkids to fit into any of your pre-conceived notions.

Fortunately, there is a bright side to consider, too. Some stepparents who have cared successfully for stepkids of this difficult age started slowly, yet eventually became important confidants—in times of trouble, their stepchildren went to them whenever they feared retribution from a parent. Such a role can be crucial to your stepkids' development and give you a strong sense of fulfillment.

What is the secret for achieving such a trusted position with people as wary as pre-teen or young teen stepchildren? Hold back and try not to expect much from them right away. Never be judgmental. Work on being an open-minded listener, a neutral sounding board.

✦ *Be flexible.*

Establishing and enforcing rules is difficult in most parenting situations, but you have unique limitations as a stepparent. Your authority does not stem from biological ties; there is no set reason why your freedom-loving stepkids should listen to you at all. In addition, pre- and young teens may be in their own personal limbo. They are old enough to be aware that your relationship to them is ambiguous, but too young to be able to handle the ambiguity maturely.

Before you get down to being someone who sets rules, therefore, you have to win your stepchildren's respect. Literally, you need to show them why they should listen to you. You have to present yourself as somebody worth their attention because of who you are apart from your stepfamily role—not because of what you say in that role.

No trick is involved; you just need to display some time-honored adult qualities. Show self-sacrifice and self-control. Be patient, forgiving, kind and polite. Respect your stepchildrens' concerns, interests, and need for "space" and time with their friends. Be non-judgmental—don't belittle their experiences or struggles as they make their respective rites of passage. Be as generous as you can with your resources and time. Appear self-assured yet flexible.

Expect your stepkids to test you and to make some mistakes as rules are set and enforced. You should not be afraid to say no, but avoid being quick to get angry or to jump to conclusions. Kids this age start to explore their debating skills, and it is likely you will to have to weather some questioning and other forms of rebellion by your stepkids. Do not take them to heart; most kids this age, no matter their family structure, challenge their parents.

♦ *Be you—not a substitute for the outside parent.*

Some stepparents mistakenly try to put themselves at the center of their stepkids' lives by attempting to substitute for an absent mom or dad. Their methods can vary. Some try to build themselves up by knocking others down, openly criticizing their partner's ex-spouse. Others discourage reminders or discussion of the absent parent at home. Still other stepparents go to extremes: they either impose themselves as rigid authoritarians or they become lax enforcers who, needing approval from their stepchildren, are willing to let just about anything go unpunished. You may feel drawn to one of these ways.

Kids this age can definitely seem like they could use a caring parent, but giving in fully and blindly to the temptation to be that person would be playing with fire. Though needy, your stepchildren can also be acutely sensitive about their past and wrestle with serious loyalty questions. If you try to replace the outside parent, you will do nothing to endear yourself to your stepkids and may, in fact, antagonize them. In addition, if you openly criticize your partner's ex, you could damage your stepchildrens' self-esteem, which could be pretty fragile already. Rather than focusing on the absent parent, work on creating your own distinct relationship with your stepchildren and have it result from how well you actually relate to each other.

Start small and build up gradually. Begin by responding to some of your stepkids' interests with approval and enthusiasm. You need not try to do everything as a family; instead, work on spending time together with just your stepchildren. Start with exclusive but limited exposure to each other and modest goals. Take a walk or watch TV together. Try not to get discouraged—results will take time. Proceed quietly but deliberately.

Be mindful of who you are dealing with, too. This children in this age group, perhaps more than any other, are the loudest denouncers of phoniness. For this reason, it is not surprising that pre- and young teens are frequently the protagonists in stories where kids reject adults who try to be something they are not.

Physical Displays and Scapegoating . . .

Frequently overlooked, the following issues can also be of concern when you stepparent pre-teens and young teenagers:

- *Use discretion when engaging in romantic physical displays with your partner.*

This issue clearly reflects how stepparents and stepchildren can be at odds on a subject. Fresh into a remarriage, charged with romance, you of course have urges to show your feelings toward your new spouse. In front of the kids, you hug and kiss with the abandon of a lovestruck couple. As enjoyable and satisfying as this may be for the adults, however, it may make stepkids turn red—and see red.

Some may value the displays as a respite from the rancorous adult behavior they knew before your new union ever developed, but many may not. Why? Young teens are at the age of puberty, a time when they are self-conscious about sex. Affection between the adults in a new stepfamily may embarrass them. They could view it as inappropriate for people "your age." And despite your partner's complicity, you alone could be the villain in your stepchildren's eyes. They may not have accepted you yet, anyway, and your romantic displays could become a focus for further criticism.

In addition, they may resent your displays because they are obvious reminders that you are happy, but they are not. And it may be hard for them to watch a parent be affectionate with someone other than their absent parent—someone they do not love and may, in fact, consider a stranger. To them, romance with a stepparent could equal a betrayal.

This issue may take on added intensity,and numerous additional complications, if you are not married to your partner and the children still live at home. For example, it may make it harder to counsel your stepkids against engaging in pre-marital sex, especially if they do not respect your non-marital living arrangement. At a fundamental level, your behavior might stir up their confused feelings even more, serving as a vivid, painful reminder of the upset and ambiguity in their lives. For all their rebelliousness, stepkids this age need well-defined structure and stability at home.

Be discreet until your stepchildren have time to adjust. A moderate show of affection will be okay—it *will* be good for your stepkids to witness expressions of a healthy, loving relationship. To avoid tension and conflict, however, save the heavy hugging and kissing for the privacy of your bedroom, or times when the kids are away.

✦ *Don't turn your stepkids into scapegoats.*

Understandably, teenage stepchildren may seem like the one true source of your frustrations as a stepparent. Teens have many good points, but they can also be very irritating and hard to handle. Yours may be careless, forgetful, disorganized and irresponsible. They may reject adult control and do as they please, talk back, play loud and obnoxious music, waste money, spend hours on the phone in seemingly idle conversation, dress funny, sleep whole days away, pursue foolish interests and embrace weird values. In short, they can act much like you acted at their age.

But in stepfamilies, there can also be a twist on the age-old story of friction between adults and teens. As they develop, your stepkids' looks and manner may begin to resemble an outside parent's. You could get annoyed with your stepkids just because they remind you of the past you want kept from your new life. No matter how difficult stepfamily life becomes, though, you must never vent your frustrations on your stepchildren. Many times, blaming them for whatever you think is wrong will be the easiest thing to do—and the hardest to undo.

Using your stepchildren as scapegoats will solve nothing. You could become resented and stiffen your stepchildren's defensiveness. Also, you could undermine their self-esteem, which may be weak to begin with. You will not be dealing with the true sources of your frustration.

The solution? Try to be moderate and discriminating. Think of the overall context of your stepfamily's circumstances. Does blame really lie solely with the isolated actions of your stepchildren? Are you upset for other, more substantive reasons, such as finances, the general—and understandable—ambiguity of stepfamily life, the difficulty of your outsider status? Is your spouse proving an ineffective leader in enforcing discipline? If so, perhaps the two of you should talk and see if you can work more closely together to improve the situation.

You are going to have to be understanding enough to give your stepchildren a break, too. One way is to recall what you were like when you were a teen . . . do you remember? What was most important to you? Were you on time? Were you scheduled? Were you serious? What did you feel? Do you recall how your parents reacted to some of the things you did?

In truth, there will be times when you will have reason to get frustrated and upset the way parents do when young people are at their worst. You never have an excuse to be expedient and resort to scapegoating, however. Because stepparents are the adults, it is your responsibility to stay calm and rational, determine the true source of your frustrations, and then address them constructively.

Remember, though, that your teens must adjust to step-family life in addition to dealing with major personal development issues. For any child, this is quite a burden to bear. Within reason, tolerate the error of their ways.

✦ *Have a sense of humor.*

Too often, humor is the last tool parents think they can use when caring for pre-teens or teens. Unfortunately, many well-intentioned yet humorless people would not last long as stepmoms and stepdads.

Nonetheless, many stepparents assume that, with teens in the house, they must grit their teeth and prepare for one unpleasant and unnerving development after another. After all, with stepkids this age, trouble comes on fail-safe tracks leading straight to a stepparent's front door, right?

"Teens? You have *teens*? Oh, boy . . . ," is the kind of reaction many stepdads and stepmoms get—not exactly a shot of encouragement.

The one-sidedness of this attitude, the absolute unwillingness to believe that your parenting experience will be good, can predominate and foster a self-fulfilling gloom and doom prophecy.

Not all children are the same, though, and yours might turn out to be different than you think. They could *appear* difficult because you have gone along with convention, decided they are trouble and settled into that approach. In this way, your negative attitude could bring the worst out in them.

A sense of humor will prevent you from making such mistakes—and refresh you as you stepparent. It will tide you over should your stepchild misuse the car or get one too many ceaseless phone calls. Humor will help you treat teen behavior as something other than the end of the world.

"The key to parenting teens? Just live through the experience," one stepmother advises, chuckling wisely.

"You will make it if you tell yourself that the kids will be gone in a few years anyway."

This stepmom's refreshingly light observation speaks volumes about the value of maintaining a sense of humor. She may find herself in an adverse situation, yet she can laugh, with a nice touch of ironic humor. Somewhere along the line, this stepmother discovered a key secret about parenting young people: by not taking matters so seriously, reservoirs of precious energy and intentions will remain in ample supply. Also, she adds that precisely because she does not let herself get caught up in daily upsets, sheis able to keep her eye on the more encouraging big picture—the relationship she enjoys with her husband andthe reasonably good job of stepparenting the couple is doing together.

You can apply humor many ways in the stepfamily setting. Think about occasionally making your points with your stepkids in light ways, for example. Write your concerns in a funny card or an amusing note. Or forget about making any points and just take your stepchildren out for some fun. See a comedy at the movies or spend a day at an amusement park. Rent an old sci-fi thriller or play some video games together. Within reason, let your stepkids' carefree teenage ways run their course.

If you mix levity into your parenting style, your stepchildren may accept and listen to you more readily. Humor will make you more approachable and interesting. You will become more than a boring adult with a monotone, always acting the same, saying the same old things in the same old ways. Stepparents who get in the rut of just having serious talks or encounters with their stepkids risk turning them off quickly. Vary your approach—a dose of light-heartedness here and there will do wonders.

Granted, not everyone has a knack for humor, but side-splitting, laugh-a-minute comedy is not required. Deep down, just about everyone can laugh at themselves if they just muster the courage. That, too, is an important application of humor in stepparenting. Instead of getting frustrated, find some amusement in the fact that, of all the things you could be doing on a Saturday, you are trying to remove a teen from bed, a task that gains urgency as the sun rises, reaches its zenith, then begins gradually descending on another day of stepparenting.

If you suddenly find yourself inside the yawning generational gap between you and your stepkids—you run out and buy them a CD in touch with *your* tastes, out of touch with *theirs*—and they look at you like you have just lost your mind, laugh at your presumptuousness, rather than getting miffed. If you are out with your stepkids, shrug off their wild teen style of dress as "kids being kids," rather than taking it as affront to your own viewpoints.

Caring for pre-teens and teens is not easy for stepparents. You are going to make mistakes and your stepkids are going to act up. In the long run, though, you will be much better off if you learn from your experiences and then shrug them off with a laugh. Perhaps your stepchildren will be nearby to enjoy what they hear—the warm sound of a very human stepdad or stepmom.

MIXING TWO SETS OF STEPCHILDREN

Mixing two sets of stepchildren has its potential pluses and minuses. For the child who yearns for brothers and sisters, acquiring stepsiblings can be a bonanza, especially if they are the same age and have the same interests and compatible personalities and attitudes. During this very uncertain stage of their lives—the formation of a stepfamily—they have friendships going or great new playmates in their stepbrothers or stepsisters.

Meanwhile, in the big picture, stepsibling relationships can be important, too. A recent study at the University of Nebraska revealed that while stepsiblings may not feel as obligated to each other as do biological siblings, they also may be less distant with each other than once believed. The results of that study revealed that stepsiblings stayed in touch with each other into adulthood with surprising frequency.

How many stories do we hear about brothers and sisters in big families enjoying each other's company and sticking up for each other? The answer is fewer and fewer, simply because many families that size have vanished. Yet, it is quite possible for such tales to emerge from well-adjusted stepfamilies with two sets of stepchildren.

Surely, you want the same sort of benefits for the kids you parent. To make them possible, however, you must be aware of the potential pitfalls first. Merging kids can bring stresses and strains to stepsiblings and stepparents alike. Adults need to be careful and thoughtful.

You should not be swayed by any myopic dreams of having one big happy family. Don't blithely assume that stepsiblings will somehow take to each other. That may never come to be. You and your partner have to weigh what your stepkids are like and plan for the real daily adjustments they are going to have to make.

For new stepparents, a big step in the right direction is to look at all of the children as individuals—not "just kids." They differ in attitude, personality and interests. This will make mixing them more delicate and complicated than you expect. Let us take a very simple example— one where just two kids are "blended"—to illustrate how and what some of the differences can be.

Grace and Bobby are about to become stepsiblings. Yet, Grace is in no mood to gain a brother—or any sibling, for that matter. It pained her to lose her birth family and she is slowly warming up to stepfamily life. Reunification of her parents remains her burning hope.

However, Grace has other concerns as well. She is very protective of her interests and what belongs to her. Post-divorce life has been difficult emotionally, but in her mother's household, Grace has had free use of two things: the car and the phone. She doesn't like the idea of sharing them with anybody, let alone a stepsibling, someone she doesn't even know.

In addition, Grace is very self-conscious about her budding sexuality. She worries that her privacy will be invaded in the new household because Bobby will be around. The adults don't expect them to use the same bathroom, do they? This is Grace's most pressing concern.

Bobby is a different story. Unlike Grace, he doesn't have strong feelings about the new stepfamily. His mother died when he was very young and he hardly remembers her. He likes what he knows of his soon-to-be stepmother. She helps him willingly with his homework and takes him shopping for clothes—something his dad has never seemed to have time for.

Bobby doesn't pay much attention to the major change that is coming. Perhaps it is because he is easy-going and doesn't need much. Bobby's biggest everyday concern about his homelife is that the television and VCR must be free so he can watch action movies and play video games. "What problems?" Bobby might say, if asked how he foresees his relations with Grace, his new stepsibling.

The above example is just one of many possible stepsibling relationships, yet it suggests how great the variances in stepchildren can be. Those differences can matter significantly when stepkids become stepbrothers and stepsisters.

In Grace and Bobby's case, the biggest difference has to do with the loss that is leading them to live together in the first place.

Grace endured divorce and still longs for her parents to reunite, so she is entering stepfamily life reluctantly. She expects everything to be difficult and glumly foresees having to tolerate her new stepfather's son. She becomes defensive whenever talk of having stepsiblings arises.

Bobby, on the other hand, is more accepting. He honors the memory of his mother, but he is indifferent about gaining a new family and a stepsibling. He doesn't expect to have problems getting along with anyone. Unaware and unsophisticated about Grace's negative attitude, he has no idea that she sees him as a threat and is poised to complain about him for very little reason.

We know that on a typical day in the life of virtually any family, siblings tangle over issues such as the use of the TV, the bathroom, the phone, the car, bedroom locations and sizes, and parental fairness. Believe it or not, that is the good news. All brothers and sisters have their spats. Arguing to some extent seems to be a pastime of their being related. This means that you will be able to ascribe some of the conflict you witness to common sibling rivalry and let it go, allowing the kids to work things out for themselves.

The bad news is that no matter the age, gender, and number of stepsiblings involved, they will likely wrestle with a troubling ambiguity which can stifle their relationships and intensify their disagreements. They may feel heavily burdened because to them, all at once, they are being asked to not only to share, but also to share with strangers.

For stepsiblings in general, very basic questions beg for answers: "Who *are* those other kids? What do they *mean* to me?" These questions arise because there are no biological ties or common histories to tell stepsiblings how to relate to one another, how to forgive and forget, and how to be and to remain loyal to one another.

Under peer pressure to have the "perfect" family, some kids may be bothered by having to explained their step-relationships to persons outside the family. They may get embarrassed when stepsiblings show up at school or on the social circuit. They may even try to escape the confusion by denying that they have any stepbrothers or stepsisters at all. This kind of denial can lead to more upset and hurt, or just stall the development of stepsibling bonds.

There are other challenges as well. Growing up with a stepsibling of the opposite sex can create a lot of confusion among kids, especially if they get along quite well each other. Interest in having sexual relations could develop.

Favoritism charges can be another big stumbling block along the way to stepfamily harmony. Stepchildren may accuse stepparents of purposely slighting them and always siding with their own sons and daughters. Some stepparents may be guilty of this or at least favor their own kids subconsciously.

The reverse may also be true: fearful of overstepping their bounds, stepparents may be lenient with their stepchildren, but not with their own children, thus drawing the ire of their sons and daughters.

Fingerpointing of every variety can be constant and intense.

"You let your kids stay up late," your stepchildren might cry. "If *we* watch TV a minute past curfew, you get mad!" In number and pettiness, such charges can be boundless.

No choice will necessarily quiet in-house critics. If you decide to pay more attention to your stepchildren, you could veer into equally choppy waters. Suddenly, your own children may feel victimized. Your son might resent any interest you take in your stepdaughter, for instance.

"What?! "You're helping her with her homework?" he might cry, coming upon the two of you working together. "You never did that with me!"

You, on the other hand, may feel guilty and confused trying to sort out and allocate your loyalties and energies.

"Should I see to my own children first?" you might fret, "or should I pay more attention to my stepkids for the sake of family unity and to prove my even-handedness?"

Another issue to consider is that stepchildren may have trouble being displaced by the age order of your step-family. For example, a child could go from being oldest to youngest and regard the drastic switch as a sudden, bitter disappointment. For many children, their place in the age ranking determines their role in their families. It says a lot about who they are.

The child affected by this type of change might have complained about having too many responsibilities before. On the other hand, he also got rewarded and took a singular pride when adults called upon him first to help out.

"What now?" he might wonder as his new stepfamily forms and he is wearing the strange and ill-fitting label of youngest child. "What is expected of me? Do I have the same privileges I had before? I don't? Why not? I am the same, aren't I?"

Even if you do your best to take care of him, your parental job of easing all of the kids' insecurities triggered by the new age ranking may never seem to end. For there may also be the concerns of the child who, in your stepfamily, is now oldest. Her worries may stand in counterpoint.

"I liked things the way they were," she could rue. "Everybody cut me a break when I was youngest. I'm going to miss that . . .

Lastly, it should be noted that some pre-established factors may help determine the course and outcome of the mix of stepchildren in your household.

For instance, if your kids are younger, they may get along better; and, if they are the same gender, your planning may be less complicated. In that case, you won't have to worry too much about privacy when it comes to room assignments.

Age is also a factor. Pre-teens and teenagers might present difficulty. Children that old may, in a sense, feel "forced" to mix. They are more aware of their situation than are some very young children. Unlike adult stepchildren, they aren't old enough to be out on their own, unaffected by parental decisions about living arrangements. They could be particularly frustrated, too, because they are at a stage where kids strive for independence and aren't as inclined to attach much importance to family matters.

The number of children involved can also determine the success of the mixing process. If you bring together not only two children, but also their brothers and sisters, you will have quite a bit more on your hands. This includes more demands on your time and energies, and more potential for rivalries and complaints about your stepparenting.

Clearly, there are no neat and tidy answers to stepsibling questions, because mixing two sets of stepchildren is rarely a simple matter.

Here are some guidelines, however, for you to consider when the Graces and the Bobbys in your life live together under the same roof:

Right away, each adult should have a realistic talk with their children, encouraging them to give stepsibling relationships a fair chance. They should point out the benefits of such communication and note that it will take some time to work.

However, don't put pressure on your kids. Make it clear that it will be okay if they don't hit it off. Advise them to discuss their feelings before they get frustrated and resort to arguing or other misbehavior.

Reassure those stepchildren who get a different place in the age order that their worth depends on who they are and how they conduct themselves—not on some age ranking. Also assure those children that the adults in the stepfamily will treat them as they had before.

Try handling the shuffling of the age order as an opportunity to learn. For the oldest child who has been demoted in age, it is a chance to show the maturity of acceptance. For the youngest, who is due to be promoted, it is a chance to grow in responsibility. The idea is to get children who face any kind of switch to think of it positively.

This type of parental counseling is related to a point mentioned before: you and your partner should look upon all of the children in your new stepfamily as individuals. Be mindful of their personalities and attitudes. Take time to listen to their concerns, fears and desires. Remember their individuality and needs as you plan your new household.

If at all possible, relocate to a new household altogether, instead of one partner moving in with one set of kids. The arriving children may feel at a distinct disadvantage because of the strangeness of the household, local school and neighborhood. Their stepsiblings could be reluctant to share what has always belonged exclusively to them. Meanwhile, the arriving kids, driven by a heightened sense of insecurity, could grow equally difficult and resentful.

Moving to a home that is brand new for everyone would erase some of these issues. There would be no basis for one set of kids to have anything over the other.

If you can't afford to relocate, introduce and acclimate the children who will be moved to their new neighborhood and school before everyone lives together. That way their new living arrangement won't seem so foreign and unsettling. Allowing them to have friends visit regularly as they make the transition to the new household may boost their sense of security as well.

In the meantime, their stepsiblings should be encouraged to be welcoming, sharing, patient and helpful. Let them know that they have special resources to offer, such as student perspective about the local school and kids' views of the neighborhood. Tell them that you will be relying on them make the new arrivals feel at home.

One last point about living arrangements: try to give every child private space in your stepfamily household. Don't forget visiting stepkids! This will help them feel secure and give them a place to "get away from it all," if they feel the need. If bedrooms of equal size can't be assigned, set up a system of rotating rooms. It might be hard for children who were living in your new home before your stepfamily formed to be so giving. But their parent should encourage them early on, employing the tactic that the stepfamily represents a new day in which everybody is starting fresh and old living arrangements no longer apply.

No matter where you and your partner decide to live, you should have all of the children in your stepfamily meet and spend time getting to know each other prior to moving in together. Set up some joint activities. For instance, have the kids play with toys and games that require a small group of children, or encourage older kids to enjoy some sports together. Have them actively share their histories by exchanging photo albums or family videotapes.

Whatever the activity is, the emphasis should be on interaction, not competition. While you don't to want to force anything, you also don't want to see the kids in situations where they don't have to open up to each other, or can put each other down.

Also, help the kids decide among themselves how they want to refer to each other. Is it brother and sister? Or stepbrother and stepsister? Something quite different? This will be a small but important way of bringing stepsiblings closer, easing early stepfamily ambiguity and preventing hurtful or tense situations.

Without any decision on this matter, stepsiblings may fail to publically acknowledge their relationship out of confusion or sheer laziness about figuring out what to say.

They might refer to a stepsister or stepbrother in an unacceptable way. "*Don't* call me your sister!"

So strive for some sort of mutually accepted reference. It will keep awkwardness from being misinterpreted as meanness or indifference, and preclude fights sparked by references that are presumptuous.

Perhaps most importantly, it will signal the opening of a very basic line of communication which will hopefully lead to substantive and rewarding stepsibling relationships.

Until a trusting atmosphere develops in your household, each adult should lead in the parenting of their own child or children, especially when it comes to discipline.

This will reduce or even preclude complaints about favoritism. It may also help if couples go over house rules with all stepsiblings present. They should explain the reasons for the rules, and stress that they represent the wishes of both adults.

When it comes time for discipline and kids from each side of the family are involved, it may be better if you don't know what the real story is to punish everyone equally, even though blame isn't equally shared. Staying neutral is key. Singling out one child could just fuel complaints of favoritism.

When young children fight, for example, a good technique is to simply confine all concerned to separate areas for a cooling-off period. That may inadvertently "punish" an innocent party, but the punishment is mild and the stepparent is spared the difficult exercise of trying to figure out who said what to whom and when. That type of investigation can be hindered by the kids and may prove nothing conclusively.

You can also protect yourself from being cast as the bad guy if, when applying discipline, you present it as the will of the adults in your stepfamily and for everyone's sake—not as something personally directed at the child in question.

Another tactic is to deal with conflict humorously—perhaps exaggerating some of the reasons for it to illustrate its foolishness. Disarmed by humor, some kids may back off and stepsibling tensions may ease altogether.

If some children constantly cry persecution in the face of house rules and discipline, you might want to suggest having regular family gripe sessions to vent their frustrations and more actively demonstrate your commitment to fairness.

Under all circumstances, however, the couple needs to make clear that, while they are interested in the childrens' opinions, they are the ones who are in control, set the rules and determine discipline. They must not allow themselves to be used as a weapon or manipulated by either set or both sets of kids.

A final point about discipline: a certain amount of misbehavior is going to be a given. No matter what techniques you try, there is still going to be some fighting or rule breaking. So don't get frustrated when you can't wipe out disputes altogether. In fact, they may not diminish until one or some of the children in your family mature and realize that their stepsiblings aren't so bad after all, and that they would rather get along with them than fight.

The same goes for favoritism charges. One of the most common causes of sibling rivalry is perceived inequity on the part of the siblings involved. You may be on the receiving end of such charges in any case. Some children will be oversensitive and create mountains out of molehills, or they may think they can break up your fragile stepfamily with their complaints. Confronted with every piece of evidence to the contrary, they will still cry foul.

Recognize such behavior for what it is. Don't pay undue attention to it or let it undermine your self-confidence as a stepparent. The upshot of this all is that you should not allow yourself to feel guilty and react whenever your stepkids cry favoritism. Judge situations case by case. Listen and learn, but stick to your guns if you think you are right.

Partners in couples need to be mutually supportive as well. When a child is charging one parent with favoritism, it is important for one adult to back up the other. This is an effective way of deflating accusations that one stepparent is being personal.

Preclude and erase temptation by setting up living situations which do not encourage incest between stepsiblings. Place stepsiblings in bedrooms which are an appropriate distance apart and which can be easily monitored. Allow for ample privacy, too. Enforce rules which call for modesty and restrict the times stepsiblings spend alone together or in each other's rooms. Also, plan parent-monitored group activities for the kids to diffuse some of the sexual attraction between the two children concerned.

If you sense a sexually charged atmosphere developing, don't ignore the signs, hoping they will go away. They can be deceiving. Expressions of strong feelings—negative as well as positive—may be symptoms. Something like, "I can't stand her! (him)" may really be said to cover or defend against being attracted to a stepsibling.

Try to elicit the childrens' feelings through an open and honest one-on-one talk with a parent. One tactic might be to frame the discussion as a health lesson. It may save on some embarrassment and be received better than a lecture or accusation.

In any case, use the session to tell them that their feelings are normal, given the nature of their relationship, living situation and stage of development. However, explain and stress that there is a big difference between being attracted to each other and *acting* on their feelings. Of course you should discuss the consequences of acting —from the broad ones like damaging their personal development and that of your stepfamily and relations with the stepsibiling in question—to more immediate ones, such as the threat of sexually transmitted diseases and the possibility of a pregnancy and their obligation to be responsible in that case. If you fail get to through and the problem persists, you may need the intervention of a professional counselor.

You and your partner are going to have to decide for yourselves what works best in your circumstances. Certainly, the ages of the children involved will be a major factor. You will probably have more control over the situation if they are young. Younger children will be more likely to consider themselves brother and sister and develop the sense that incest is taboo.

On the other hand, parental control and clear cut answers may be harder to come by if the children are older or even young adults. To put it bluntly, could you accept stepsiblings in their twenties sleeping together? Whenever stepsiblings are attracted to each other, the answers to such questions will come from your own attitudes, your understanding of your stepchildren's relationship, and your judgment of its impact on them and your stepfamily overall. There have been cases where stepsiblings who don't live together strike up love interests in each other and the adults involved don't make a big deal out of it.

Yet, the fact remains that you and your partner are the ones who determine what is permissible for the kids living your household. If sexual relations between stepsiblings are not allowed and make you uncomfortable, your stepchildren need to respect that. If they can't, and they are old enough, perhaps it is time for them to move out.

You are bound to feel differently toward the sets of kids in your stepfamily. You may love your own, but not your partner's. That is okay—and normal. The important thing is that you adhere to a parenting style which values communication and is fair, honest and thoughtful.

Those same qualities should also characterize the way relatives treat the children in your stepfamily. You don't want a situation where one set of children is constantly being remembered or doted on by certain relatives with gifts and attention as the "real children," while the others are ignored or made to feel as though they are second class citizens. Such a discrepancy could be a source of hurt, conflict and division. You and your partner need to encourage extended family members and friends to treat all the children in your stepfamily equally as much as possible.

Unfortunately, some stepparents practice equality in only the most superficial of ways. For example, when their kids are clearly in the wrong, acting up against their stepsiblings, the stepparents let it go, in effect using their own children to work out their hostility towards their stepkids. You should not let yourself fall into this practice or do the reverse—allow your stepkids to get away with murder because of your guilt about your ambiguous feelings towards them.

It won't help for you deny to your stepchildren that your feelings towards them are different from your feelings towards your own children. However, if you are truthful, be sure to add—and mean—that you are trying to do the best job possible of parenting in the case of every child in the family.

Don't get frustrated if one child does not want to assume the role of a stepsibling, thereby putting a wrinkle in your hope for family unity. Be patient. Do not give in to fits of temper or emotion. Instead, calmly keep sight of what is best for each child in your stepfamily. Not all children will adapt the same to the many changes that come with stepfamily life.

It may be very tempting for some couples to simply concentrate on caring for their own children. Confronted with all of the early ambiguity and confusion of a new stepfamily, that choice can appear much simpler to new stepparents than trying to break ground caring for a second set of kids whom they don't know.

Stepparents who make that choice, however, could permanently curb the development of family unity if they aren't careful. If they unwittingly choose to interact only with their own kids, they could in effect, set up a house divided.

Such actions may also be personally harmful. Imagine the reaction of your stepchildren if you fall into the rut of always praising or talking about your own kids, but never have anything positive to say about your stepchildren whom you've allowed to remain as strangers to you.

Ultimately, everyone in your new family must get along in order to have maximum success. It is best if you help to achieve this as soon as possible. If nothing else, you will set a good example for your own children. Why should they get involved with people whom they see you ignore?

Don't be afraid or lazy. Parent and engage in a relationship with your stepchildren appropriately. Start slowly, increasing your involvement gradually and steadily.

Parenting two sets of kids is a balancing act. You must be involved, but you also must not overparent. Couples should give children room to develop their relationships on their own—they should not be "forced" to get along by adults. You want the kids to bond because it is beneficial and because *they* desire it, not you just you.

Don't lose hope prematurely. Stepsibling relationships take time, and there will probably be plenty of rough spots. Make sure you distinguish between those which reflect the difficulties of stepfamily life, as opposed to pure sibling rivalry, and those which represent both. Remember that competition between stepsiblings is not necessarily going to have a negative effect. It can encourage to try different roles and help them to discover how they want to relate in the new stepfamily.

In the end, it is likely that a less than perfect bond will develop between stepsiblings. You should accept those imperfections. Stepparents would be foolish to expect the children to relate as biological brothers and sisters. That does not mean, however, that they will have something less—only something different.

A bit of perspective may help reassure you, too. In one sense, any compatibility between and among stepsiblings is an accomplishment in light of the mixed histories and many challenges of stepfamily life which have to be reconciled and overcome. Be happy about that.

Remember, too, that the couple's actions—not the stepsiblings'—is the foundation of the stepfamily. You and your partner will have a very good chance of succeeding at stepparenting if you remain unified. Your devotion to each other will help to strengthen your ability to deal with stepsibling spats and other pitfalls.

Couple unity can filter down to your advantage in many ways. If the children come to realize and appreciate the fact that you are happy, they may drop their guard and be more open towards their stepsiblings.

"Why not?" they might say to themselves after awhile, consciously or unconsciously. "Mom (or Dad) seems pretty happy. Maybe there is something to stepfamily life after all."

AND BABY MAKES . . . ?

As you settle into stepfamily life, one of the biggest choices that can confront any couple may eventually arise: whether or not you and your partner should have your own child.

It may surprise and encourage you to know that many couples successfully integrate a new baby into their stepfamily. In the face of pre-existing child care responsibilities and despite having broader stepparenting issues tugging at them, they manage to provide a setting which benefits the newborn and strengthens their stepfamily.

Few would argue, however, that successful integration does not require forethought and planning. As a caring stepparent, the last thing you want to do is have a child blindly and realize too late that it was the wrong decision.

Unfortunately, some couples have the wrong motivations. They think having a baby will erase all of the ambiguity and uncertainty in their lives, quickly bringing their stepfamily closer. Everybody will bond around the child, they think—it can't help but be the event that finally unifies us.

Also, some couples just see having a child as a way of cutting ties with unhappy pasts rather than as a major commitment to the future with real responsibilities that can wear on a marriage if they aren't dealt with properly.

Insecure stepparents, especially those who have never had children, might push to have a baby because they think it will alleviate their loneliness as singular outsiders or permanently bind their spouses to them. Others might pressure their partners for a child because they feel like they are "owed" for parenting stepkids, or because they want children, but can't deal with stepparenting.

Quite simply, having a baby does not "save" stepfamilies just as it doesn't save marriages. True, having a child can be beneficial; it can distract stepfamily members from some nagging concerns, rally them around childcare issues and imbue them with happiness and pride. None of that will be enough, however, if your stepfamily has fundamental flaws—for example, if you and your partner don't parent as a team or if there has been a failure to openly discuss and resolve loyalty and loss issues pertaining to the past.

Without question, you and your partner need to give plenty of thought to this issue. Introducing a baby into your stepfamily can be fraught with complications. The children you already have may resent a newborn. The youngest ones in particular may feel insecure as the fuss over the baby builds and draws attention away from them. In addition, they may misinterpret the birth as a sign that they are not good enough for the adults.

The list of things which might feed such feelings goes on. For example, your stepchildren could become self-conscious because their surname is linked to the past—an unhappy time in the adults' lives—while the baby's reflects your bond to your partner with renewed hopes for a brighter future.

Also, the baby could symbolize a permanent break with a past the children hold dear; to them, its birth could even represent a betrayal of the outside parent. Age order issues may crop up, too. A baby's arrival will automatically displace the younger kids in the old ranking, a development which they might find unsettling.

Meanwhile, stepparents can wrestle with their own issues, especially if they have never had children before. To you, the baby could be your "real" child and its birth could radically temper your interest and involvement with your stepkids. Consequently, you could suffer guilt pangs, or feel severely conflicted in your feelings towards the children in the family.

At a basic level, having a child may prove to be just plain disruptive. Responsibilities and challenges are inherent to stepfamily life. Do you really want to add to them significantly by having a baby? What about child care arrangements? Your financial resources? Could your stepfamily afford to have one adult stay home with the newborn? What will having a child do to your housing situation? Do you have room for a nursery? Are the other kids in your stepfamily going to accept curbing their behavior—tiptoeing around in deference to an infant, or having their sleep disrupted when the baby fusses?

Here are some tips for making the birth of your child an ideal event—one that will reflect you and your partner's mutual love and stand a chance of winning acceptance from your stepfamily while strengthening it at the same time.

✦　✦　✦

Have the child for the right reasons—and be realistic about what its impact will be on your stepfamily A newborn is not going to necessarily improve a stepfamily or reduce its ambiguity. In fact, it may become a focal point for division and confusion among your stepchildren if you and your partner don't take some precautions. Give your decision plenty of thought and make sure it is not driven by insecurities over any of the relationships in your family, including your marital one.

✦　✦　✦

Timing is a very important factor. Couples who opt to have a child shortly into the life of their stepfamily risk adding a new complication before some old ones have been worked out. You may want to wait to have a child until your family members generally feel more secure and more accepting of each other.

✦　✦　✦

Involve your stepkids as much as possible in the birth. Make the baby's arrival a true family affair, not something which is just between you and your partner.

Early on, perhaps as soon as mother begins to appear pregnant, start preparing the stepchildren. Reassure them that you have enough love to go around and that the coming of the child will not diminish your love or interest in them. Assuming they are old enough, you may want to make your stepchildren feel like they have important active roles to play as big brothers and big sisters. Impress upon them that you will be depending on them during the change that is ahead, and that the new child is going to look up to them.

With all children, you want to make the baby seem real—not some abstraction that they could take as a threat. Engage them by having them help pick a name for the child or involving them in child care. Look for some extra steps to take that will help forge a bond. For instance, prominently display pictures of all the kids together, or encourage your stepkids to give the newborn a special toy they had as infants as a symbol of the connection between them. And when your stepchildrens' birthdays roll around, give *them* something special on behalf of the baby. The basic idea is to make your stepchildren feel included and important—which they truly are.

✦   ✦   ✦

Be prepared for and accepting of the impact the birth will have on your feelings for your stepkids. Like many stepparents, you will probably feel very differently about your own child than you do about your stepchildren. No doubt you will love your baby automatically, something which in all likelihood never happened with your stepchildren. Your newborn will be free of the ambiguity which can muddle relations with your stepkids. Also, the child will be associated with a newer and brighter stage in your life.

When they realize this split exists, stepparents should not feel guilty. It will be quite normal for you feel closer to your baby. You need now perceive your divided feelings as a sign of failure or inadequacy in you or your stepchildren. However, because such conflicts do arise, stepparents should consider delaying having a child until their stepfamily relationships are secured.

Love your child, but keep on trying to develop your bonds with your stepchildren, too. Do not become so taken with your newborn that you ignore your duties towards your spouse and all the children in your stepfamily.

✦   ✦   ✦

Make practical preparations for the childbirth. Obviously, there are practical steps to take in advance for your newborn. You have to tend to such things as picking a name, making sure you have an adequate supply of baby products and writing your child into your wills and your insurance coverage.

However, practical considerations must also extend to your stepchildren. Well before the birth of your baby, listen to what they have to say about the potential practical impact of the birth on them. Assume that they have some valid opinions and will not just accept the changes in the daily life of your household, especially if your baby is born while your stepfamily is young, relationships are undefined, and your stepkids are tired of dealing with upheaval and change.

Time management will be a key issue once the baby arrives. For instance, if you have weak relations with your stepchildren, how do you plan to strengthen them while you also care for your newborn? You and your partner may want to recommit yourselves to involvement with your stepkids. Schedule regular times with them and stick to them. Make it a point to attend their school functions or to participate regularly in their interests and activities, however limited your participation must be.

A birth could also adversely effect your "couple time"? This precious togetherness—your mutual sessions renewing your relationship, planning, letting off steam, relaxing, discussing and agreeing upon how to handle problems—is the engine that will pull your stepfamily forward. You need to figure out how to sustain it amidst all the uproar of caring for a newborn.

If the woman ends up doing more babycare, her partner has to be understanding, not resentful, about his lost time with her, and be as helpful as possible instead. Several arrangements are possible. One partner's parenting of the older children may have to increase as the other one focuses more on the baby, for instance. Key in this situation is that each adult appreciate the impact of the new demands on the other and the couple find a way to stay in close communication.

Ideally, you will be living where a baby can be added without much disruption in room arrangements. If it is necessary to reorganize space, however, give your stepkids a voice in how to do this. Make sure they know you will keep their wishes and comfort in mind as you rearrange.

On a broader level, you should review the impact the birth will have on your finances and, indirectly, your care of the children you already have. Can you pay for childcare? Can you or your partner afford to stop working and stay home with the baby? How will baby-related expenses affect what you are able to do for your stepchildren?

Encourage everyone to try to look at these practical issues as opportunities, not problems. Present the baby's birth as a chance for all family members to cooperate as care providers. There is no guarantee your stepchildren will join in, but the likelihood is increased if you engage them as valued support, rather than alienating them by simply handing them duties or excluding them from planning.

PART FIVE...
OTHER CONSIDERATIONS

HOLIDAYS AND SPECIAL OCCASIONS

Stepparents admit that holidays can be rough for the unaware and unprepared. Many dread their coming, looking upon them as "something to get through," rather than the joyful and pleasant occasions they should be. Why?

Holidays can do a powerful job of eliciting stepfamily ambiguity and division. At these times everyone's family may seem close and loving—except yours.

You can be overwhelmed with feelings of profound loneliness, isolation and frustration if you are not prepared. Hurt, but blind to the fact that your stepfamily is acting normally and cannot and should not be measured against biological families, you can start to seriously doubt its chances and your own ability to handle stepparenting.

"It was a disaster," is one stepmom's succinct description of her first Christmas with her stepfamily. "I bought gifts for my stepchildren, thinking we would have a special day. "But one didn't even bother to open what I had gotten him, and another didn't like his gift and gave it back. I thought their behavior was rude, and I fought with my husband about it."

Unfortunately, this stepmother harbored hopes that did not take her situation into account. Even though her stepfamily was new, she thought everyone would want to be together and get along, matching perfectly the ideals set for holiday family behavior (elevated notions which biological families often never meet, even though they are free of stepfamily pitfalls).

Her disappointment was almost too much for her to bear. "I drove to a shopping center lot and sat there in my car, feeling like the holidays had blown up in my face," she says, recalling her bitter disappointment.

Fortunately, she and her stepfamily recovered and stayed together. Did she learn anything from her trouble? "Have very low expectations about holidays and be clear about your plans. The key is to be creative and flexible. The more rigid you are, the more upset you'll have."

Other stepparents say the same things. They talk about having trouble dealing with a range of concerns, from decisions about where the kids should spend dinners and how to handle gift giving, to their own expectations of their stepchildren during holiday times. Issues that simmer all year often boil over as loyalty questions come to the fore.

Meanwhile, stepchildren can have a rough time, too. Yours could be insecure or resentful about feeling as though they have to participate in unfamiliar holiday traditions. This may become a flashpoint for heated disagreements.

"Rituals are part of what they are," one counselor noted, discussing how stepchildren feel their way along at holidays. "They want to hold on to them."

In addition, stepchildren could feel like they are playing second fiddle to stepsiblings if they live together. Shuttling between households, they could become confused about their loyalties, overwhelmed by the multiple celebrations of various family segments, and sad and guilty about their outside parent.

"It's really hard when you leave at 2:00 P.M. on Christmas Day, and tell her, 'Have a fun day,' when you know she is going to be by herself," is how a stepdaughter once explained her feelings about a visit to her mom's.

There are many ways to handle these holiday worries, though. First of all, stepparents must keep their expectations realistic.

The divisive ambiguity in your stepfamily knows no holiday. It is going to be with you on Christmas, Chanukah or any other special occasion, just as it will be at all other times, or perhaps even more so.

You should not expect too much of your stepkids—you cannot force gaiety, expecting them to be easily warm and sharing, or to think solely of you. If they do, consider their actions a bonus. The holidays may be as rough on them as they are on you, since they, too, have to deal with and decide about divided loyalties and unfamiliar settings and customs. Instead, cope as best as possible, comforting yourself with the idea that holidays should become closer, more easily managed affairs with time.

You can help bring on those days by anticipating holidays and discussing them openly in advance with your stepfamily. Respect your stepchildrens' traditions and try to honor them as much as possible, but give thought to developing some new ones for your new stepfamily, too. Encourage with words such as: "Despite what you think, we do have something in common: this is my first holiday with this family, too, and I'm feeling a bit lost, just like you. But can't we put our heads together and figure out if we can't come up with some new ways to celebrate?"

Start small. Be satisfied if one or two new tradition-setting activities go reasonably well. They can always be increased and developed. Plan for holidays together. Celebrate by going out for dinner, or by preparing a meal at home. (If a home-cooked meal is the choice, have everyone help. Besides fostering a greater sense of togetherness, it will spare harried stepparents extra and unfair pressures.)

You could blend some of old with some of the new, too. Celebrate in a manner preferred by your stepchildren. Whatever you decide, such activities can lay the foundation for closer bonds and develop your stepfamily's sense of identity, in addition to saving the holiday from being a miserable experience.

As you set the stage for the future, remember to take some precautions for the present—safeguards that will protect you from crushing disappointment. Devote at least part of your holiday to you partner and yourself instead of making a complete emotional investment in your stepchildren. A special dinner or gift exchange between couples that tells them they are appreciated and doing just fine as stepparents can be a sweet offset to whatever your stepchildren do—or fail to do.

♦   ♦   ♦

It is also important to try to cooperate with the other household. Instead of brokering a peace, warring adults can use holidays to intensify their battles. Unfortunately, kids usually end up the biggest losers in these cases. The last place stepchildren need to be is in the midst of holiday bickering. The upset can cause lasting damage to their emotional and psychological health.

Solicit your stepchildrens' wishes in a way that does not make them feel like their loyalties are at issue or that everything hinges on what they say. If they want to spend the day with their mother or father, accept this rather than taking it as a personal insult.

"We understand how you feel, and will try to work something out" is better than an accusatory, "What? You don't want to spend the holiday with us?" Such reactions can induce harmful guilt in your stepkids.

If possible, set up mutually acceptable dinner and visitation schedules with the other household in advance. As always, you must be flexible and forgiving. Tell yourself you are strong enough to put up with one day of inconvenience, even if it is a holiday, and that cooperation is worth it if there will be minimal arguing and general satisfaction.

✦　✦　✦

Even if the other household is uncooperative, stay calm. Rather than reacting to grievances—the other household's conflicting dinnertime and irresponsible mixups shuttling the kids between households, for instance—have the attitude that you can work around obstacles and celebrate the holiday your own way anyway, with a bit of imagination and creativity. Set up alternative dates for a family dinner, or begin a tradition that belongs just to your stepfamily. Come up with a special time for family members to gather and make their own holiday decorations together, to be photographed as a family or to listen to grandparents relate some family history. Steps like these will enable you and your mate to retain control of the holiday observance and keep yourself from being at the mercy of an uncooperative household.

✦　✦　✦

Be reasonable about gift-giving. It may happen, yet you can't expect your stepchildren to come to you bearing gifts. The very idea could violate their sense of loyalty toward their absent parent. Even if another parent is not involved, they may not feel comfortable giving you something because of the new, uncertain nature of your relationship. If you must, take the pressure off your stepkids by saying in advance that it is not necessary for them to get you anything.

You, on the other hand, should not try to "buy" stepchildren with presents. If you take it upon yourself to get what *you* think they want or need, your effort could backfire. You could end up seeming interfering, disapproving, or out of touch. Instead, get to know your stepkids and what they like first. Then get them something that, within reason, reflects what you learn. Do not be surprised if you don't get an enthusiastic response or even a "thank you" for your trouble, either. Sometimes, because of their strong sense of attachment to the past, stepchildren have a hard time showing any acknowledgment towards or connection to a stepparent. Or they may just be unappreciative the way kids can sometimes be, which you may not be used to if you have never been around children.

Above all, be fair. If two sets of kids are in your house, treat each the same—as much as possible—in order to minimize competition and resentments. If relatives are kind enough to give your stepchildren gifts, make sure the children acknowledge them. Their failure to do so could get your stepkids off on the wrong foot by leaving bad first impression.

Another problem which could arise is conflicting gift-giving styles. Your stepchildren may be used to receiving expensive gifts, and that may no longer be possible in the scaled back economy of your new stepfamily. To preclude any disappointment and hurt, your stepfamily should discuss and agree on gift-giving practices openly and honestly. Your stepchildren will be much better off in the long run if they generally know ahead of time what to expect.

And stepparents beware! Do not accept your partner and your his or her ex-spouse buying gifts together for your stepchildren. This behavior could falsely signal their reunification and diminish you in your stepchildren's eyes, blurring the boundaries between families.

Certainly, reasonable gift-giving is a nice touch at holidays. Gifts can be great symbols of how much the giver cares about the recipient. In a stepfamily, they can help establish ties when appropriate. Remember this key point, however. If your relationship with your stepchildren is going to work, you will have to make an effort to connect daily in a lot of other ways which are more critical and more difficult than handing out presents. You can not buy your way into stepparenthood. You should not expect your stepchildren to bond with, let alone love you, simply because you give them nice things.

◆   ◆   ◆

Remember to celebrate. More than anything else, holidays may make you a self-conscious stepparent. You should not let self-criticism sway you into saying that those days are only for "real families." Be more positive. You and your stepfamily *are* a real family. Even though you lack biological ties. You have to be understanding and respect your stepchildren's feelings about their natural parents and former lives. You have to accept standing off to the side, so to speak, when their attention shifts to an absent parent on certain holidays.

However, none of this erases the fact that very important stepparenting is going on, courtesy of your good efforts. So celebrate and take pride in this achievement; it qualifies you to think of yourself as belonging to the ranks of dads and moms everywhere. Of course, the same broadmindedness should apply to your stepfamily, too. You have every right to think of yourselves as a family and to feel good about participating in family holidays.

It is understandable if the holidays, and their accompanying advertising campaigns, caused you to feel like an outsider. Unfortunately, media and commerce, lagging well behind the times, contribute to stepparent alienation.

Despite the rising stepfamily population, they still fail to recognize stepparents to the extent they should. By this neglect, they further the fantasy of "traditional" families—whoever *they* are.

A light shines here and there, however. For example, the Stepfamily Association of America has voted that the first Sunday in October each year be designated Stepparent's Day, and many states have pushed for the observance. If it is on the calendar where you live, make sure you celebrate this day! Contact local stepparent organizations and get involved in observances. Find out how you can promote such a holiday and bring more recognition to stepparents and stepfamily life. It is much needed.

GRANDPARENTS

Next to parents, grandparents are often childrens' major adult figures. Ideally, they are loving, available and generous. For lucky grandchildren, birthdays, graduations and holidays mean toys and envelopes with money. Also, there are the many times grandparents serve as babysitters or chaperons, taking their grandchildren to destinations such as amusement parks or the zoo.

But there is much more to being a grandparent. A storehouse of information about the past, grandparents represent the family foundation. They tend to the subtle but important task of solidifying their grandchildrens' place in the world. When a divorce occurs, they are often called upon to serve as anchoring influences for their children's families. Often, those on the custodial side of a divorce settlement get even more involved with their grandchildren than they otherwise would.

Perhaps grandparent issues are not a problem in your case, especially if your stepgrandchildren are quite young.

Research says that stepgrandparents do eventually grow into typical grandparenting roles and kids do manage to see grandparents and stepgrandparents pretty much the same way (again, the younger the children, the better).

Nonetheless, stepparents also say that problems can emerge. Ambiguity and uncertainty can touch extended as well as immediate stepfamily members. Confused, grandparents on either side could desperately wonder how to relate to their stepgrandkids. Overprotective and fearful about "losing" beloved grandchildren to a remarriage, grandparents on the non-custodial side may try to impede your stepparenting or target their stepgrandchildren for ill will. Some grandparents have been known to dote on grandchildren, but to ignore stepgrandchildren, sending resentments reverberating throughout stepfamilies.

Meanwhile, the children under your care may be cool and distant, too. Insecure and rebellious, they could be indifferent towards step grandparents, or fail to respect or appreciate them.

◆   ◆   ◆

Amidst the disruptions of getting settled, new stepparents often overlook the impact their stepfamily may have on grandparents—and vice versa. As a stepparent, you cannot afford to be that way; you will only increase the chances that relations with grandparents will hinder rather than help your stepfamily. You do not want to miss the opportunity of having the support of grandparents in a stepfamily situation. The continuity they represent can help grandchildren to adjust amidst the uncertainties of stepfamily life. Also, grandparents can fill in occasionally as child caretakers for harried couples. (However, stepparents must be aware that thoughtlessly "dumping" the kids at grandma's is out, for instance. She has a life, too.)

The following are some guidelines for ensuring that, when it comes to grandparents, the bases are covered. Provided the contact is healthy, reassure all grandparents, paternal as well as maternal, step as well as biological, that you welcome their relationships with all of the kids.

◆　　◆　　◆

If one set of grandparents and grandchildren is very close, make sure they know you will not stand in the way. You cannot allow yourself to feel threatened. Instead, think in terms of what is in the best interests of your step-children. Their relationship with their grandparents could be a precious, important and comforting link with the past —an emotional security blanket—that they want and need in order to cope with the uncertainties they face as new members of a stepfamily.

◆　　◆　　◆

Be patient, yet proactive. You should not "force feed" stepfamily life to anyone. Your spouse's parents or your own, fixated on one family type, could resent your new life, thinking it somehow reflects negatively on them. They may regard it as a break in the family line and worry about inheritance issues. More immediately, they may be con-fused by change and be at a loss to relate. They may not yet understand that they are not expected to love their step-grandchildren, only respect them.

"You can't make somebody love somebody else," one stepmom observes, discussing the subtle tactic she thinks is best for grandparents. "Openness and flexibility on every-one's part is the best policy."

Researchers say that non-custodial grandparents, in particular, tend to feel cast aside when couples part ways. They feel 'left out' and 'forgotten' after a divorce and fre-quently experience negative emotions and grief over the loss of their grandchildren." A journal reported some years ago, "These results support the trend toward grandparent visitation rights . . ."

If this is true in your case, the parents of your partner's ex could try to put you in a bad light with your stepchildren. You may have to take it upon yourself to try to mend fences by initiating a difficult outreach or by putting up with some unsettling contact with them.

Meanwhile, the younger generation may show similar behavior. For many reasons, your stepkids may be cool and distant with stepgrandparents. They could be bothered because they have no love for them, unaware that their feelings are normal and that all that is needed at first is respect. They may also think that getting close would betray their grandparents. Furthermore squabbling adults could manipulate them into being antagonistic.

Grandparents and stepgrandchildren will need time to adjust to each other. There is much to resolve; it would be unrealistic to think grandparents will have the same regard for stepgrandchildren that they have for grandchildren—and vice versa. They need a chance to establish and develop their relationships on their own and in their own terms.

As a stepparent, you can be an important, soothing intermediary, though. One idea would be to invite each set of grandparents over to explain some of your stepfamily's history to the kids. It could set the stage for bonding and erase some of the children's insecurities by giving them a fuller understanding of the past.

Some other tips: make sure all grandparents have a schedule of all the kids' birthdays and school events, send them stepfamily photos and update them regularly on the general family news. Encourage them to visit, and visit them.

Meanwhile, have your stepchildren try some small touches, such as sending a birthday card to their stepgrandma or a get well card to their stepgrandpa, or thinking of their stepgrandparents with cards and gifts at holidays and birthdays. Have them invite them as well as their grandparents to their school functions. Encourage them to visit the older folks if they live nearby.

You can draw the line on behavior. While you should give relationships a chance to work themselves out, you need not put up with everything that develops as older and younger generations try to work things out. Right away, for example, you and your partner should let it be known that you prefer to have all of the grandparents practice equal treatment within reason, and that you expect your stepkids to respect all of your stepfamily's relatives.

This could mean that grandparents and stepgrandparents alike give all children the same kinds of gifts. It could also mean that, at your request, they should not go to any lengths to differentiate between sets of children in social situations. For example, they may pointedly say "*step*grandchildren" when introducing your children to friends, long after the distinction is necessary. If you and your partner have decided that all the children in your stepfamily are simply "the children" or "the kids," the reference for stepchildren could come off as insensitive and divisive and be taken as a hurtful slight by your stepkids.

Regarding inheritances, grandparents have the right to grant them to whomever they wish, though the giving will obviously be better appreciated if it is done with the best of intentions and not out of spite. If they do want to leave something for stepgrandchildren, they should consult with professionals about amending their will to make sure it refers specifically to their stepgrandkids. An ambiguous, loosely drawn will which only talks about "my children and their children" or "my grandchildren" could be contested or executed to exclude stepgrandchildren, even though that may not have been the deceased's intention at all.

Stepparents do not have to accept the behavior of grandparents who transfer their unhappiness to innocent stepchildren by ignoring them, making a show of treating their stepsiblings better, or by turning their grandchildren—your stepkids—against you. Grandparents may have the right to feel the way they do, but they don't have the right to interfere with, divide or otherwise mistreat members of your stepfamily. If they do act unkindly, the person whose parent or parents are causing the trouble should lead in raising the issue and trying to talk things out.

Be open, honest, understanding, forgiving and firm. One possible approach could be saying, "Look Mom (or Dad), I know that our new family may be difficult for you to accept. Yet, I have to ask you not take your frustrations out on the children. They haven't done anything and your behavior is harmful to them.

"We love you and always will. In the future, could we discuss your frustrations openly and honestly and figure out a way to resolve them rather than feeling hurt or being hurtful?"

Another approach could be to say, "Mom (or Dad), you are so important to the success of our stepfamily in so many ways. Because you gave me a lot of love, I can be a loving person for my stepfamily. The kids really need you, too. They need the same love you gave me as well as having as many good examples from caring adults as possible as we adjust to stepfamily life."

It may help to introduce grandparents to other stepfamilies in order to show them that yours is not so odd after all. Another sensitizing measure could be to have them attend community education classes for a basic under-

standing of stepfamily life. If you suggest that, be diplomatic. The older generation may resent having the younger
one tell them they need some education. It might help to
propose the classes for everyone's edification—encourage
not only grandparents to attend, but also as many other
members of your stepfamily as possible.

If grandparents continue to be unhelpful, or even
destructive, it may be necessary to declare a "cooling off"
period during which everyone stays away from each
other. This should be a last resort, done in the interest of
everyone's good, rather than spite. It may seem drastic, but
you will fare better in the long run if you and your partner
stay united and committed to each other.

Likewise, although the children need not warm up to
all the grandparents concerned, they should respect
them and not go out of their way to make them feel like
outsiders. Parents should take the lead in sensitizing their
own children to the grandparents' feelings. The following
quotation illustrates just how this is possible.

"That person (your child's stepgrandparent) may not
mean a whole lot to you right now, but they do mean a
lot to my husband (or wife), your stepparent, so they mean
a lot to us. I am asking you to respect that. Also, if you will
just be patient, you may discover that your step grandparents are very nice and that it is possible and not a
betrayal of your biological grandparents to have a good
relationship with them."

Part Six...
One Step Ahead

Now matter how many books you read, the challenges awaiting you as a stepparent will not disappear. In fact, as soon as you put down *You're A Stepparent... Now What?*, you could be immediately thrust into one of the numerous crises of self-confidence which deflate the energy and optimism of many well-intended stepparents.

Once again, you could feel unsettled, even guilty, convinced that something inside you prevents you from falling head over heels in love with your stepkids and they with you.

You could again feel trapped and powerless because you mistakenly moved into your new partner's house, when you should have chosen a neutral site as your step-family home.

You could be either overbearing or skittish about disciplining children who "aren't really yours." Remember "Bobby", our stepson composite from earlier chapters? In the next moment, he could lean into the doorway of your living room, hand extended, wanting more money. Meanwhile, Grace, his older female counterpart, could rush out of the house without saying anything to you, looking like the last person on earth capable of recognizing what you do for her.

There is always the threat of a nasty little stepsibling war, too. Bobby and Grace could erupt, taking out their stepfamily insecurities on each other, upsetting your dreams of family unity.

In another example, a perplexed grandmother—your mother—could soon phone, wanting to know "just how should we refer to ummmmmm . . . what's his name (your stepchild)?"

The stepparenting road is not a short, straight, clearly marked path across the terrain of the heart. It zigs and zags, doubles back, twists, turns, and can make you feel like you never left point A—and will never ever reach B.

The ups and downs are really not the issue, however. They will always be there. It is how you deal with them—how you choose to travel—that is the question. Hopefully, after having read this book, you are more sure of yourself than you were before. In these pages, you should now feel like you have a basic but useful mental compass to guide you on your stepparenting journey.

♦   ♦   ♦

Before you head around the next bend in the road, here is a brief recap of some key points to ensure that your journey is a success:

Have realistic expectations—forget about comparisons and perfection. Do not rush to see everything settled quickly; it takes years for members of stepfamilies to become adjusted to each other, and not everyone adjusts on the same schedule.

However, time by itself will mean nothing unless you, your partner and your stepfamily members each work at making your stepfamily a success.

Be aware, too, that your enthusiasm and views about your new stepfamily may not be shared by your stepchildren. They are in their own worlds, which are probably far apart from yours. Thus, you cannot approach stepparenting expecting stepchildren to fulfill your needs—your wish for a child of your "own," your strong desire for your "own" family, etc.

Stepchildren have needs, too. Their immediate concerns could well include wanting their biological family back or feeling obligated to be distant with stepparents out of loyalty to their absent parent. At the least, you should head into stepparenting aware that there could be this discrepancy.

Remember that couples are the key to successful stepfamilies—you and your partner need to make a *constant* effort to communicate and be mutually supportive of each other. Once you talk things out and have set yourselves firmly as the foundation of your stepfamily, strive to be as open and communicative with your stepchildren as possible. Usually, it is most effective to present decisions as joint ones and to relay them in advance. That will give your stepchildren time to understand and accept what you want, plus they will get the clear message that they can not divide and conquer because you and your partner are so unified.

Aim for respect, not love, in your relationships with stepchildren. Age and gender will be important determinants in how you and your stepkids relate. However, it is best to approach them with open-mindedness and on an individual basis.

In general, stepparents should focus on modest goals such as spending some time exclusively with their stepchildren. If this sounds disappointing, take heart; over time, stepparents can become very important adult figures in the lives of stepchildren. Sometimes, deep and loving relationships even result.

You have to take the right approach toward step-parenting; you need to practice acceptance, patience and flexibility. Thinking and living by in absolute terms, such as setting your sights strictly on being a parent in the traditional sense to your stepchildren, is probably not going to work. Broaden your thinking and be willing to tolerate your stepchildren's view of you, not the image you think you project.

Several kinds of roles—mentor, aunt or uncle, good adult friend—are also options for you to consider. They may turn out to be the better choice, depending upon how you and your stepkids hit it off.

You also need to be generous—not necessarily financially, but in terms of giving time, interest and energy to your stepchildren, with no prospect of immediate return.

In other words, over a very big heart, you need a very thick skin. Like natural parents, you are going to have to overlook a lot, yet, because you are not tied biologically to your stepkids, you are going to have to work extra hard to forgive and forget. "Super empathy" is required of stepparents, an expert once noted.

Keep the proper perspective on the absent parent. Do not try to replace or compete with him or her, or be predisposed to criticize or do battle. You want your relationships with your stepchildren to be positive and to be strictly about you and them. Criticizing absent parents can be the biggest mistake stepparents make. It can hurt their stepkids' self-image; also, stepchildren with a strong sense of loyalty to their parents can be deeply offended by the criticism.

Parents, not stepparents, should take the lead in disciplining their own children. Before you can be an active disciplinarian, you have to earn something more than your stepchildren's perfunctory respect. Until they know you and trust you better, you can't expect them to listen to you simply because you are now the new dad or mom in the house. In their eyes, you could very well seem like just another adult—not someone who deserves automatic obedience.

However, while your partner should apply discipline whenever possible, you should also have a say in what the rules are. These rules should be presented as the wishes of both adults to keep you from being perceived as a villain and a target of retribution from your stepchildren.

Be proud of being a stepparent. It has been pointed out in this book that stepparenting is not easy, but there is a difference between something being difficult and something being negative. Is stepparenting hard? Yes—it can be described as station that pressures people to relate, rather than letting their relationships simply emerge.

Can there be problems? Yes. Even serious ones? Yes. According to a 1993 National Research Council report, "Adolescents living in either single-parent families or in stepfamilies are far more likely to engage in risky behavior, including running away from home, dropping out of school, smoking and truancy."

Nothing is a given, however, there *are* many happy and fulfilled stepparents and stepfamilies. Much will depend on your outlook and your choices—whether you decide to keep your chin up and make the best of things or hang your head and give in to frustration.

Hopefully, because you have read this book, you will be in a better position to make correct choices about stepparenting and increase your chances for success.

RESOURCES

Of course, it would be nice if the secret to successful stepparenting could be summed up neatly in a closing summary. As a stepparent, there is so much to learn. Stepfathers must be patient with the tight mother-child bonds they are likely to encounter. Stepmothers should avoid the trap of the "Supermom syndrome," or being shocked and discouraged by unappreciative stepchildren. Also to be considered are the special concerns that go with parenting visiting stepkids, stepsiblings, stepfamilies in which a newborn is added and grandparents on all sides of a remarriage. The practical issues that should get your attention are figuring out what to do about names, giving adequate thought to where you will live, and addressing the need for advance, organization in a stepfamily's financial planning.

By no means do you and your partner have to "going it alone," though. Although you may not know any of them, millions of people are heading down the same road that you are. Meeting and talking with other stepparents in a support-group setting may be ideal for helping you to gain or just maintain strength, confidence and perspective. One good way to meet others like you is to get in touch with the Stepfamily Association of America, 215 Centennial Mall South, Suite 212, Lincoln, Nebraska 68508-1834. Tel: 402-477-7837.

Founded in 1979, the Association is a non-profit educational organization which maintains a national network of local stepfamily chapters. Coast-to-coast, they run informal discussion groups that are perfect settings for anyone interested in getting a sincere, caring, friendly and knowledgeable hearing. Chapter socials are opportunities for stepparents and stepfamilies to meet and enjoy each other's company.

The Stepfamily Association also publishes a newsletter, holds an annual meeting, and distributes books on various aspects of stepfamily life, some geared toward specific age groups of children.

Be wise enough to reach out for help if you need it. Some issues may seem bigger than they actually are, and can be put in the proper perspective with assistance from a counselor. Also, counseling can help you anticipate many problems, preparing you to deal with them before they lead to great upset.

Depending upon your needs, a counselor may be a psychiatrist, a psychologist or a layperson with experience and training in working with stepfamilies. Contact your local community mental health center for leads on finding the appropriate one for your situation.

Bear in mind, too, that counselors periodically hold seminars, teach courses and host discussions on stepparenting and related issues. Check your local paper, human services department, non-profit clearinghouse, mental health center, library, continuing education office, or community center to find out about those near you.

✦　✦　✦

For further reading, you may want to try these helpful books:

How to Win As a Stepfamily, by Emily B. Visher and John S. Visher

Stepfamilies Stepping Ahead: An Eight-Step Program for Successful Family Living, edited by Mala Burt and available through the Stepfamily Association of America.

♦   ♦   ♦

In recent years, the size of the stepparent population has far exceeded expectations. Will these numbers continue their dramatic rise? Nothing is certain. It is the case that a society-wide brake seems to taking hold: in mid-1993, for instance, the Census Bureau reported that the national divorce rate was stabilizing along with "many of the social changes that redefined family life in America," according to the *Washington Post*. The aging of baby-boomers was cited as one of the major reasons behind the slowdown. They were thought to be reaching an age group where divorce is less likely.

However, while that development may temper the stepfamily population's rate of growth, it hardly means that stepfamilies will decline in significant numbers, or that yours will stick out like a sore thumb, conspicuous for its makeup. The lingering effects of past trends alone may keep that from happening. According to the *Post*, the Census Bureau's mid-1993 report "showed that the idealized married-couple family with two children, has not constituted, at any time in the recent past, a majority of American households."

As recently as 1992, the Census Bureau still estimated that four in ten marriages would end in divorce (a forecast revised down from five in ten). Meanwhile, the outlook for attitudes about stepparenting seems much more nebulous. On one hand, you can feel comfortable about getting on with stepparenting more openly. For example, gay parenting and marriages are coming into the public eye more, single and unmarried couple parenting have both been on the rise and partners' customary roles have continued to blur and be redefined.

Working moms are now commonplace and women are more independent-minded and less reliant on men then in past decades. Meanwhile, ideas about male parenting keep changing, prompted by everything from shifting attitudes about what male household duties should be, to the interest more and more fathers are expressing in winning custody in divorce cases. Stepparents are basking in the limelight that comes with social change and illuminates one message very clearly: never put too much stock in what others think.

"They seem more interested in owning the term [stepparenting]," observes a therapist, comparing your generation of stepparents to people she counseled years ago. "Nobody used to talk about it before. It's akin to 'coming out of the closet.' People are more willing to identify themselves with step titles, and they are more matter-of-fact about being stepparents. It is a nice thing to see."

Indeed, there seems to be little time for much worry about whether one's form of parenting matches social convention. Increasingly, quality of parenting is considered to be more important than appearances. Now more than ever, the world seems to be crying out for better care of its children.

Key institutions and settings for teens—including families, schools and neighborhoods—have "come under siege" over the past twenty years, declared a 1993 report by the National Research Council. This was just one more finding in an already long string of discouraging reports that seems to keep unraveling at an ever increasing speed: stories about increases in child abuse, juvenile crime, school violence, poor academic performance by students, television-saturated teen pregnancy and suicide, adolescent substance abuse and risk of HIV infection, and kids and parents who are woefully out of touch with each other.

In late 1992, the Carnegie Council on Adolescent Development said teens spend an average of five minutes per day in one-on-one interaction with their fathers and about 20 minutes of such time with their mothers. On the whole, the Council reported, many adolescents have a great deal of discretionary time, "much of it is unstructured, unsupervised and unproductive for the young person."

♦ ♦ ♦

Yes, there has been all this, plus dozens of tales by the dozens about the heavy time and financial pressures that weigh upon so many working couples these days— pressures that hinder their ability to parent effectively. Against the relentless drumbeat of bad news, what seems to matter as you head into tomorrow is not whether you are a stepparent, but whether you are willing and able to be responsible, caring, interested and involved with children. Hopefully, the signs of open-mindedness will predominate and society will welcome you.

Although some people may be slow to recognize and understand who stepfamilies are and what they need, family structure in this country has been going through tremendous change for some time. This development is so pronounced that it prompted one pair of social observers to coin the term "multiple-option family." They explain the term as meaning that family makeup today, "comes in all shapes and sizes."

While strides have been made to improve perceptions of stepfamily life, there is still a long way to go. Rather than pursuing "sociological stereotyping, we need to explore the varieties of stepfamily experience," researcher Frank F. Furstenberg, Jr. urged not very long ago.

A voice of reason and clear-thinking, Furstenberg called for more research less labeling. "What are the conditions that promote successful relations between stepparents and their children?" he asked. "Are there distinctive styles of stepparenting that seem to be associated with favorable outcomes for children?" He also noted that "An important area for research and policy analysis is what factors might promise a greater level of cooperation between parents after divorce." No matter how many calls there are for ending stereotyping, however, some amount of it will continue. At this writing, Hollywood is probably hard at work producing yet another movie about a psychopathic stepfather with a blood lust, kids are absorbing the video images of Cinderella's wicked stepmother, and journalists are using the word stepchild as a negative metaphor in stories for tomorrow's papers.

As a stepparent, you must not pay attention to or be daunted by these and anti-stepfamily portrayals and practices in political, legal and media circles. Collectively, subtly, they can infect stepparents with self-defeatism. Despite these influences, though, many stepparents still find self-fulfillment plenty, while managing to live up to the belief one insightful stepdaughter put nicely into words: "Children," she noted, "are entitled to be cared for by kind, loving adults who are not only parents to them, but friends as well."

Can you be the kind, loving person so many stepchildren seek? Of course you can, and the way is clear. Good stepparents know that success means being tolerant and participating in an endless, constant process of re-examination, renewal and recommitment. If you are going to do things right, you will have to join with your stepchildren in mutual exchanges, outreaches, rejections, victories, defeats, achievements and frustrations.

Every stepparent stumbles and falls. Successful ones find ways to pick themselves up again and again—ways that often include calling on others for help. If there is one secret to successful stepparenting, this may be it.

Now the next bend in your stepparenting road is just ahead. It will not throw you, however, for you have already taken a step in the right direction—not a bad way to begin your future.